Stephan Dubreuil

Come Quick, Danger
A History of Marine Radio in Canada

...---...

Ship to shore, do you read me anymore,
This line is bad, and fading,
Ship to shore, answer my call,
Send me a signal, a beacon to bring me home;
Chris De Burgh

© Minister of Public Works and Government Services Canada — 1998
Available in Canada through your local bookseller or by mail from
Canadian Government Publishing – PWGSC
Ottawa, Canada K1A 0S9
Catalogue Number T31-107/1998E
ISBN 0-660-17490-1

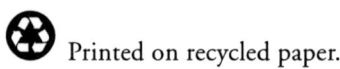 Printed on recycled paper.

Acknowledgments	vii
Foreword	ix
The Wireless Wizard	1
The "Big Thing"	4
Mulock and Smith	5
Republic and CQD	7
The Laurentian Region: They Came Out of the Backwoods to Build a Radio Station	11
Rivière-au-Renard	13
Grosse-Île	14
Pointe-au-Père and the Empress of Ireland	15
Cap-aux-Meules Coast Guard Radio	18
Sept-Îles	18
Rivière-du-Loup	20
Newfoundland and the *Titanic*	21
London Radiotelegraph Conference	26
Safety of Life at Sea (SOLAS) Conference	27
Cape Race, Newfoundland	27
St. Lawrence and Comfort Cove	28
St. Anthony	30
St. John's	32
Stephenville	33
Calling Nova Scotia	35
In Action	38
Transatlantic Communications	43
Halifax Radio VBQ	50
Post-war Camperdown	50
The Italia	51
Radio Stations Combined	52
The End of Manual Scanning	54
Human Distress	55
Rum Running on the East Coast	58
Yarmouth	63
Sydney and Charlottetown	65
Halifax Coast Guard Radio	66
Radio and the Great Lakes System	67
Thunder Bay	69

Port Burwell	70
Point Edward and Sarnia	71
Radiotelephone	72
Toronto and Cardinal	76
VHF (Very High Frequency)	77
The "Ghost"	79
The Sinking of the *Aigle D'Océan* and the Arctic Region	81
Nottingham Island	85
Cape Hope's Advance	87
Iqaluit	88
Inuvik	89
Resolute	90
Point-to-Point	92
Untin Bowler and Point-to-Point	93
Voice Broadcasts	94
Killiniq: Returning to the Old Haunts	95
The Pacific Region	101
Marconi Loses the "Shoe-in"	102
The First Decade	105
Triangle Island	108
Bull Harbour and Comox	109
The End of Dead Reckoning	111
Radio Broadcasting	114
Interference Call	115
Estevan Point and World War II	118
Vancouver / Women Join the Team	119
Safe Passage—Clean Seas: Marine Communications and Traffic Services	121
Ecareg and VTS	122
Québec	126
Montréal	127
LORAN	128
DGPS	129
Suez, Supertankers and MCTS	130
100 Years of Service	131

Acknowledgments

In producing this book, I discovered that writing about history requires more than simply exploring pertinent facts and myths. It also means grappling with the totality of the subject at hand. As well, I learned that the "new frontier," often evoked in the context of the United States' past, is also entrenched in Canadian history. As the frontier matured and changed with each foot forward, so too did the Canadian psyche and identity take shape. Not unlike the major leaps of ages past, 20th-century technology continually marches forward. But this time, the pioneering path is peopled by men and women I have been fortunate to meet. I visited some of these pioneers in their homes and, over coffee and across the kitchen tables, heard their stories. Not all of these accounts are related in these pages, but many a good tale has found its way in.

As I began plotting my course for interviews and research leads, no doubt impossible without the help of Henry Phillips, Chief of Training & Human Resources at the Coast Guard's Marine and Communications and Traffic Services (MCTS), I soon found the task daunting, urgent in fact. Those pioneers of the technology age were, one by one, passing on. As my work progressed, I was shocked more than once to discover that someone had died, just days before our scheduled meeting. I regret that I never got to meet these individuals and that they never had the opportunity to recount their marine-radio experiences for this book.

I would especially like to thank radio operator Spurgeon G. Roscoe for taking the time to sit with me and share his fascinating experiences. His unpublished manuscript on marine radio in Nova Scotia serves as a backdrop for the "Calling Nova Scotia" chapter. In the same vein, radio operator Jean-Pierre Lehnert's support was invaluable in gathering information about the Arctic region. Thank you also to W.J. Wilson, retired Director-General of Telecommunications Regulation, who shared his insight into accounts from the Great Lakes region. My appreciation also goes to the people at the S.P.A.R.C.[1] Museum in Coquitlam, British Columbia.

---

[1] Society for the Preservation of Antique Radio in Canada

The idea to produce this book issued first from Lea Barker, Director of MCTS, Canadian Coast Guard. Many thanks go to Lea. A special thank you also goes to the people at MCTS for providing me a wonderful work atmosphere and for taking the time to answer my many questions. I would also like to express my gratitude to the library personnel at Transport Canada and the Department of Fisheries and Oceans for their valuable assistance. I spent several months rummaging through their numerous stacks of annual government reports.

My friends and family were also extremely supportive. I especially thank Robert Murray for his moral support and, most of all, for his advice and for the time he spent editing my early drafts.

Of course, a special thank you goes to Marconi himself for the history he gave us and, incidentally, for the title of this book. The Marconi Company's wireless distress signal CQD took effect February 1, 1904. CQD in Morse is "_ . _ .   _ _ . _   _ . .". The CQ really meant "Stop Sending and Listen" and the D was later interpreted as "Danger." The popular interpretation of the call was "Come Quick, Danger." And much like its successor, SOS, which some soon interpreted as "Save Our Souls," CQD is really part of Morse code, a universal language that stands outside of these fictional interpretations. CQ is still used today when addressing ships and stations. Given this, I found CQD a fitting title not only for its historical value but also for the mix of fact and fiction it presents.

Foreword

On November 19, 1996, radio operator Vern Hillier sent the last Morse code message from the Canadian Coast Guard Radio station at Ketch Harbour, Nova Scotia, closing an era in the long, remarkable history of Canadian marine radio operations.

This book attempts to capture the nature and history of marine communications. But communications is a field that is rapidly overstepping itself with the implementation of competing satellite communications systems, the demise of Morse code radio transmissions and the ubiquity of the cellular telephone. At this very moment, the noiseless foot of time brings with it the end of the era of the traditional radio operator.

The men and women who served in the vast network of Canadian radio stations deserve to have their dedication to safety preserved before their stories are gone forever. This determined, professional group of individuals provided an essential and comforting link to mariners off the coasts and on the inland waterways of Canada. Radio operators worked in extreme environments and in isolated locations, but always with the knowledge that their work was providing mariners with a safety and communications link to essential information, to business associates, to land-based rescue services and to families at home.

In compiling this history, Stephan Dubreuil has selected from a great volume of material the facts and anecdotes that best represent the full sweep and colour of the experiences of Canadian marine radio operators from their beginnings to the modern era. I consider this an important work. Not only is it entertaining for the lay reader and for persons interested in the history of technology, it is also a document of archival significance. I therefore dedicate this book to all radio operators, past and present.

Lea Barker
Director, Marine Communications and Traffic Services
Canadian Coast Guard

Introduction: The Wireless Wizard

In the beginning, there was just salt water meeting fresh water. Hosts of mammals and fish were drawn to this unique ecosystem—the St. Lawrence River. This was a waterway that was magnificently wild and vastly uninhabited, and whose waters knew only paddles and canoes. In what seems no time at all, all that changed.

In 1534, Jacques Cartier, driven by his quest for the Orient, cautiously navigated his vessels up the mighty St. Lawrence. Could he, a seasoned navigator, have imagined that the quick-tempered waters of the St. Lawrence, or any sea, would one day be effortlessly spanned by such a thing as wireless?

An Italian nicknamed the "Wireless Wizard" was the first to achieve just that. He was a man whose thoughtful eyes looked upon the future with the conviction that his work would one day bring safety to mariners the world over. Today's advanced field of telecommunications confirms that Guglielmo Marconi's pioneering efforts have proven worthy of his conviction.

Years before Marconi developed his wireless invention, complex manual signalling systems had been the mode of communication between ship and shore. These systems obviously necessitated that the communicating parties be in view of each other. With the advent of the numerical code, anything from flags to large baskets were used to fly a signal. Messages often took up to an hour to relay, and ships alone on the heaving sea could do little but watch and wait. It was the Industrial Revolution that spurred the minds of the first modern communications pioneers, as they grappled with the archaic systems that no longer sufficed.

In his early adulthood, Marconi began pondering the work of the German physicist Heinrich Hertz. Proving James Clerk Maxwell's theory, Hertz demonstrated the propagation of electromagnetic waves through space. The results of his experiments formed the basis of our future understanding of the behavior of radio waves. Hertz's discovery was made possible by using a high-frequency oscillator whose radiation emissions were picked up on a receiver a surprising 10 metres away. Maxwell had previously purported that any change in electric and magnetic fields would result in electromagnetic waves moving through space. Such waves are commonly referred to as Hertzian waves, with wavelengths ranging from millimetres to kilometres. Marconi was enthralled by the possible communications applications as he read of Hertz's experiments. In the years that followed, Marconi stood unremittingly convinced that long-distance communication without wires was possible.

Guglielmo Marconi was born on April 25, 1874, at his family's house in Bologna, Italy. His childhood was largely spent travelling with his elder brother, Alfonso, and their Irish-born mother, Annie. Annie's father, Andrew Jameson, and his brothers made their money in the whisky trade and founded a well-known Dublin distillery famous for its *Jameson Irish Whisky*.[2] Marconi's father, Giuseppe, was a squire at the Villa Grifone where the young Guglielmo Marconi eventually set up a laboratory.

Marconi's biographers all agree that Guglielmo was neither a success in school nor in social settings. Devising scientific toys captured his interest the most. Marconi has been described as a timid, withdrawn child. With an ever-widening rift between his parents, coupled with years of living out of a suitcase, the young Marconi was deprived of a sense of security, resulting in the reserved nature that set him apart from the other boys of his age. Marconi failed to qualify for the Naval Academy, but his supportive mother and brother encouraged him to concentrate on his scientific pursuits. His father was opposed to this advice and Marconi had to wait for many breakthroughs before gaining his father's respect and approval. In the attic at Villa Grifone, Marconi pegged away shaping his dream into a reality.

Early in summer, 1895, Marconi succeeded in transmitting signals over a distance of a few metres using two insulated plates separated by a spark gap, which consisted of two small spheres connected across the secondary of an induction coil. The primary winding of the induction coil was equipped with a battery and a Morse key, and the receiver was a coherer type. Marconi adapted the existing coherer, a glass tube filled with metal filings. More precisely, the coherer is a cell containing a granular conductor between two electrodes; the cell becomes highly conducting when it is subjected to an electric field. By adapting the

---

[2] Mary K. MacLeod, *Whisper in the Air*, Hantsport, Nova Scotia: Lancelot Press, 1992, p. 15.

coherer, Marconi was able to relay Morse code. In *Whisper in the Air*, Mary K. MacLeod tells us "he learned telegraphy skills and the Morse code from Nello Marchetti, an elderly telegraphist going blind. In gratitude for Marconi reading aloud to him, Marchetti taught him the code." By August 1895, Marconi had already transmitted a signal over a distance of three kilometres. Greater distances, Marconi discovered, could be achieved by using a ground connection and an elevated aerial at both the transmitter and receiver.

With a portfolio of successful transmissions, Marconi felt ready to approach the Italian government with his apparatus in the hopes of having it developed. But Italy was apparently not ready for Marconi. Undaunted, he set off for England in 1896 where, following the advice of his cousin, Henry Jameson Davidson, Marconi filed the world's first patent application for a telegraphy system using Hertzian waves. The patent was granted on June 2, 1896.

With the help of the wealthy Jameson family, Marconi met Sir William Preece, a scientist also concerned with the practical application of wireless. Preece held a prominent position at the post office at the time and was responsible for overseeing all aspects of communication. He proved invaluable to Marconi's research by allowing him access to the Preece laboratory where as MacLeod states, "Preece had been searching for the answer that Marconi had found."[3] In 1897, Marconi successfully established wireless communication across the Bristol Channel. Though Preece was also experimenting with purely inductive methods at the time, Marconi's system proved more efficient, setting a new record for distance of wireless transmission—14.4 kilometres. Many experiments followed and wireless transmission gained in credibility. Not long after the record-breaking transmission, the Wireless Telegraph and Signal Company was formed in London, England, on June 20, 1897, listing Guglielmo Marconi as the senior shareholder.

The first years of Marconi's company were extremely active: the Italian Navy adopted the Marconi wireless; Lloyd's of London requested a demonstration of a wireless link between Ballycastle and Rathlin Island; the press used wireless for the first time; and, from Osborne House, Queen Victoria communicated with the Prince of Wales who was on board the Royal Yacht in the Solent. Later that year, the French government granted the Marconi enterprise permission to construct a wireless station near Boulogne-sur-mer at Wimereux. In March, 1898,

---

[3] Ibid., p.41.

the French station sent its first official cross-channel wireless message to South Foreland, England, effectively inaugurating international wireless telegraphy.

Such achievements no doubt influenced then Royal Navy Captain Henry Jackson to submit a request for the installation of wireless on three British ships. The request was granted and the system was subsequently put to good use in the South African War. Marconi later travelled to the United States to report the America's Cup Races with the further intention of demonstrating his apparatus to the Naval Department. By 1900, with each success overstepping the other, Marconi seriously considered the idea of spanning the Atlantic, a project he called the "Big Thing."[4]

Meanwhile, as more and more ships were being fitted for wireless telegraphy communication, staff shortages at the stations were posing a problem. In 1901, because schools had yet to include wireless communication in their curriculum, Marconi's company opened the first wireless school at Frinton, England. Before long, engineering students were graduating with a competent understanding of Marconi wireless. To this day, students continue to enroll at the Marconi College in Chelmsford, England.

The "Big Thing"

The signal covered a distance of 3,000 kilometres from the English shores to Signal Hill at St. John's, Newfoundland. The message, which took the form of 3 dots representing the Morse code letter "S", became the first transatlantic radio signal. Just before this historic feat, Marconi ordered the construction of the station at Poldhu in Cornwall, England. Prior to this event, the Italian scientist set out for America to build a station at Cape Cod, Massachusetts.

The transmitting antenna of Marconi's system was comprised of a fan-shaped network of wires which hung from 60-metre towers. Harsh weather conditions had proven disastrous for the circular aerials originally installed at the Marconi stations, prompting Marconi to replace them with the new fan design. Drawing from the power source and high-voltage transformers housed in the operations room, the wires connected to the spark gap were charged with alternating positive and negative currents. The currents enabled a signal to be flashed across the Atlantic from North America and to be received by a similar network of wires at the Poldhu station in Cornwall, England. The wires channelled

---

[4] Ibid., p. 48.

the signal to the operations room where a magnetic detector retrieved the message.

The magnetic detector was made functional by hysterisis[5] effects in a moving iron wire; or, in other words, by the amount of magnetic energy absorbed by the wire. Marconi said that the passage of a signal across the Atlantic is practically instantaneous, an estimated one ninth of a second.

Weather conditions forced Marconi to abandon Cape Cod in favour of a temporary station at Signal Hill, Newfoundland. Unfortunately, gales were a constant challenge on the Canadian coast as well. Yet, Marconi persisted. He had previously concluded that transatlantic communication would be easier from Newfoundland as it was the closest landfall to Cornwall. On December 12, 1901, Marconi recorded in his diary that even though gale-force winds had made it difficult for he and his assistants to launch the aerial on a kite, the scheduled signals transmitted from Poldhu came in that afternoon at 12:30, 1:10 and 2:20.

Mulock and Smith

In 1896, the Liberal party came to power in Canada under the leadership of Wilfrid Laurier. William Mulock, Canada's first Post Master General, was a member of Laurier's cabinet, and it was Mulock who oversaw the success of the penny post, the Pacific cable and wireless telegraphy. He, Laurier and the Maritime representative at the time, W. S. Fielding, were having breakfast one morning when Mulock received a letter from one of his officers, William Smith. Smith wrote that Marconi was in St. John's but was unable to continue his experiments. The telegraph company there had exclusive rights to all communications in the colony and had filed an injunction to bar Marconi. The Italian inventor was said to be considering relocating to the American east coast to continue his work.

Smith had previously met with Marconi and had told him that Canada would be interested in his work. He asked Marconi to delay his U.S. plans until after the subject of wireless was brought before the Canadian government. Smith impressed on Mulock that the matter was urgent and insisted that Marconi be invited to Ottawa. Marconi, in fact, went to Ottawa and the men struck a deal. The Italian scientist undoubtedly walked away delighted because, after soliciting many

---

[5] When ferromagnetic materials are placed in a coil of wire carrying an electric circuit, the magnetizing field caused by the current forces atomic magnets to align with the field. This alignment increases the total magnetic field.

nations' help to develop his idea, none had responded as favourably as Canada had.

The Canadian government agreed to invest up to $80,000 to construct a station at Table Head, Nova Scotia, and stipulated that wireless-communication rates were not to exceed half of the rates charged for telegraphy. Consequently, rates for wireless were fixed at 10 cents a word for standard communications and five cents a word for the press, and Canada maintained rights to all monies made from messages issuing to ships from Canadian stations.

Around this time, Canada was becoming aware of itself as a continental nation and was studying the major challenge of bridging the vast distance to the west. Wireless was poised to become the principal method of communicating across the expanse of the Canadian territory, as well as within the Great Lakes. Mulock was convinced that such an efficient means of communicating across great distances would be invaluable in a country such as Canada that was bordered on three sides by oceans.

In view of the Canadian government's interest and assistance, Marconi established the Wireless Telegraph Company of Canada in 1902. The Department of Marine and Fisheries commissioned the newly formed company to build six stations along the St. Lawrence River and Gulf of St. Lawrence—more specifically, at Fame Point, Belle Isle, Heath Point, Point Amour, Cape Ray and Cape Race. Their purpose was primarily to reduce the too-frequent naval tragedies in Canadian waters.

In the pioneering days of wireless, rumours about the questionable confidentiality of wireless messages were spreading. Some telegraphers even alleged that they could discern the flashes or the letters of the messages as they lit the sky over the towers. Such unearthly occurrences as this would indeed hamper the secrecy of communicating with wireless. When a *Sydney Daily Post* reporter asked Marconi about the revealing flashes he chuckled and answered, "It must have been flashes of lightning that were seen at such a distance."[6]

Marconi was a shrewd businessman and realized that good public relations were important to protect the shareholders' investments. Marconi was so eager to protect his and the shareholders' interests that he strove to obtain an international wireless monopoly. Later, he successfully set the wheels in motion, primarily in Canada, the United Kingdom and the United States, and soon Marconi owned and oversaw the operation of each company formed in each country. Through various patents and

---

6   *Sydney Daily Post*, Cape Breton, January 12, 1903.

diverse business schemes, Marconi boldly worked to control marine communications worldwide.

Conflicts naturally arose, however, when other companies began offering identical or similar services. When Kaiser Wilhelm II, for example, attempted to send a telegram to Germany from the German Hapag Liner *Hamburg*, his efforts were thwarted because the Germany of 1905 had no coastal wireless stations. The telegram could have been sent to the island of Borkum and then to the German mainland via cable, but the Marconi enterprise refused to accept messages from any stations other than Marconi ones, and the *Hamburg* had a Telefunken station. The frustrated Kaiser set out to create a wireless station called Norddeich Radio, which started operating later that year. Marconi, all the while, held fast to the monopoly principle, enforcing a no "interstation" communication rule. This steadfastness may have cost him the contract to build a wireless network on Canada's west coast, a project later undertaken by the Canadian government.

It must have seemed to many people that Marconi did indeed have a monopoly in Canada; and it cannot be said that the government was unaware of other viable radio systems. As early as 1903, the Public Works Department maintained equipment manufactured by the American De Forest Wireless Telegraph Company in at least one Canadian station and, by the following year, the Canadian branch of the company, Dominion De Forest, had two commercial operations, one in Toronto and one in Hamilton.[7] Canadian legislation ensuring some measure of free enterprise was already in effect under the 1889 *Combines and Investigation Act*, the predecessor to today's *Competition Act* which became law in June, 1986. In fact, very little could thwart the efforts of Marconi's competitors except, of course, Marconi's own ingenuity.

Republic and CQD

On January 23, 1909, the British White Star Liner, *Republic*, outbound from New York to the Mediterranean with 460 American tourists on board, collided with the Italian liner, *Florida*, inbound for New York from Italy. *Florida* was ferrying 830 emigrants, mostly people evacuated from the aftermath of Italy's devastating Messina earthquake. But nature, this time in the form of thick fog, took its toll yet again. The operator aboard *Republic*, Jack Binns, whose wireless station was located in a shack typical of the

---

[7] Sharon A. Babaian, *Radio Communication in Canada: An Historical and Technological Survey* (Ottawa: National Museum of Science and Technology, 1992), p. 14.

time—a wooden structure fitted haphazardly on the boat deck—found his shack suddenly destroyed. With the shack in disarray, Binns sent the first CQD, the Marconi-recommended distress code, across open air. CQD was later replaced by the clearer code, SOS. Binns managed to rig a canvass to cover and protect himself from the cold while he spent most of the next 72 hours signalling a sister ship, the *Baltic*, to come to the passengers' rescue.

The English, American and Canadian press hailed Binns a hero for saving the lives of 1,290 passengers. But the incident did more than make Binns a hero. It rendered wireless a crucial and integral factor in the shipping world, securing its permanence. Following this narrowly averted disaster on the North American coast, shipping nations responded quickly by outfitting most of the world's ships with the now indispensable wireless communication technology. The *Republic* incident, however, was just a prelude to a much more publicized—and pivotal—event in international maritime history, the sinking of the *Titanic*.

It was wireless telegraphy and then marine radio which gave navigating officers "the eyes" they needed to more effectively sail the world's waters. Marconi's wish to encircle the earth with his apparatus clearly anticipated Marshall McLuhan's global village. But, as with the old marine radio stations scattered across the globe, another era is currently coming to an end in Canada. The year 1994 saw the last graduates of the Canadian Coast Guard Radio Operator training who studied Morse code. Elsewhere, the U.S. Coast Guard sent its last message of dots and dashes in 1995. Across the Atlantic, the Swedish Göteborg Radio (SAG) fell silent on January 1, 1995, after 85 years of service. Stockholm Radio (SDJ) took over the remaining traffic on very high frequency (VHF), MF and 500 kHz.[8] It is a farewell to an era pioneered by the likes of Morse, Bell, Fessenden, Marconi and De Forest in favour of more modern technologies such as automated and satellite communications.

As society advances, it does so hand in hand with technology, and the Canadian Coast Radio Service is not immune to the changes. On January 17, 1994, Coast Guard radio stations across the country began their march toward integration with Vessel Traffic Services (VTS). Many of the old marine radio facilities are controlled remotely by Marine Communications and Traffic Services (MCTS) centres. With the advent of automated communications, the marine radio of yesterday is no

---

[8] Birgitta Gustafsson, "End of an 85-Year Epoch," *The World Wireless Beacon* (Geyserville, California: Society of Wireless Pioneers, vol. 7, no. 2, June 1995), p. 6.

longer. Today, the MCTS[9] program, a new and autonomous directorate under the emblem of the Canadian Coast Guard[10], oversees all matters marine within the scope of communications and vessel traffic services in Canadian waters. With an eye on today's economic context, MCTS has had to tailor its own place, but not without the backdrop of experience and tradition.

---

[9] The Canadian Coast Guard has amalgamated its Vessel Traffic Services and Coast Guard Radio Station programs into a new organization called Marine Communications and Traffic Services (see Chapter 7).

[10] On January 26, 1962, the government's fleet of 60 ships and 181 northern service landing craft was officially designated the Canadian Coast Guard. In April 1995, the Coast Guard moved from Transport Canada to the Department of Fisheries and Oceans.

Chapter 1

The Laurentian Region: They Came Out of the Backwoods to Build a Radio Station

The rise of telecommunications in Canada is a remarkable success story. It starts with the first commercial marine radio station in North America—Fame Point. Located at the eastern tip of Québec's Gaspé peninsula, Fame Point juts into the rough waters of the Gulf of St. Lawrence. A British warship called the *HMS Fame* had run aground off the point, and the Canadian government built a lighthouse shortly after, naming the high cliff on which it perched in memory of the lost crew. A telegraph line was soon built to enable the lighthouse keeper to report the ships transiting the Gulf.

In 1904, the keeper welcomed engineer Joseph Barridon and his assistant Hugh Lyle to the point.[11] These men announced, as they climbed out of their buggy, that they were going to build a wireless station. They brought with them an idea that had already begun to make waves in the industrial and scientific world. The construction of a wireless station in backwoods Gaspé was the intent of the newly formed Marconi company. Little did the residents of the lighthouse know that they would witness some of the first glimpses of the coming communication age.

In spring, 1904, Barridon and Lyle built the station and installed Marconi's apparatus: the standard one-kilowatt Marconi spark-gap transmitter, a Marconi 10-inch induction coil serving as emergency transmitter and a Marconi magnetic receiver. The equipment was ready to go.

---

11   Lloyd Nelson, "Goodbye Old Fame Point," *News on the Dot* (Ottawa: Department of Transport, December 1957), p. 2.

Saturday June 25, 1904, 8:25 p.m., first communication with Parisian *bound east, 38.3 km west. 9:33 p.m. Finish with P. read 16, sent 1. Communication perfect.* This brief entry is the first of the original Fame Point log. It records the ship-to-shore communication that preceded all others on the continent.

With only minor modifications, the spark sets used for these communications remained the industry standard for two decades. The transmitter consisted simply of a coil coupled to a long length of wire serving as the aerial. Two rods were placed end to end on top of the set with a gap of a few centimetres separating them. When the telegraph key was depressed, electricity travelled through the rods causing a spark to oscillate from one end to the next—thus the name Spark Gap Transmitter. On the other hand, the first receivers used a coherer as the main receiving component. These sets readily reacted to bursts of static electricity which operators had to learn to filter out.

Despite the great strides in communications technology that wireless represented, there were still no defined frequency bands—you were either heard or you were not. Within a few years, as wireless gained in popularity, schedules were established and each ship fitted with these sets was allotted a certain time to transmit in a designated area. Of course, in these earliest days, no laws governed wireless except for a few regulations concerning the licensing of stations. Operators, for the most part, were landline telegraphists who chose to serve in the coastal stations. Two versions of the code were used, and operators were simply expected to use the code the coastal station operator understood.

With no laws or official jurisdiction aside from a few company instructions, the language used in wireless communications was not always meant for delicate ears. A common term was GTH—Go To Hell. If an operator took offence at such a rebuff, he simply had to flash up his transmitter for maximum power, put a book on his key and hold it down, creating as much interference as possible. At the early stages of the telecommunications era, poor equipment design not only allowed for offending other operators but, because of its considerable lack of safety, misdirected sparks often scarred operators' hands and arms.

Safety questions aside, Barridon and Lyle continued to oversee communications at Fame Point, although the station only operated when a steamer was near enough to establish reliable contact. A continuous watch was unheard of because of the limited range of coverage that each station afforded—33 kilometres. After Barridon's departure a few months later, the station was staffed with two operators and a cook. As technology advanced and wireless became increasingly popular among ship masters, the Department of Marine and Fisheries was later compelled to augment staff to maintain continuous watch.

The days of experimenting were far from over, and the move to continuous watch spelled another turning point for the Marconi enterprise. As early as 1903, Marconi opened a shop in Montréal—the first to manufacture commercial radio equipment in Canada—and, by 1909, the Marconi Wireless Telegraph Company of Canada boasted stores on both William and Delorimier Streets in Montréal. In 1904, the William Street shop was building high-frequency transformers and magnetic detectors, equipment evidently used in marine radio stations across eastern Canada, the Great Lakes and, finally, the entire nation. Today, Canadian Marconi, located in the Montréal suburb of Ville St. Laurent, produces high-technology products for the aerospace market. Along with its subsidiary company, Cincinnati Electronics, Canadian Marconi produces navigation systems, cockpit displays, satellite antennae, spacecraft transmitters, infrared warning systems and missile warning systems. General Electric Company of England is the majority shareholder of both companies.

Rivière-au-Renard

During the first 20 years of the Marconi Fame Point station, supplies were shipped from Québec City by government steamers. Sailing vessels had long been supplanted by these coal-burning wonders. Supplies were unloaded on shore and hoisted up the 45-metre climb to the station. The Gaspé region is one of horrific snowfalls, quickly burying the landscape under mountainous snow banks. Come spring, the officer in charge of Fame Point usually had to place the annual phone call to have a government bulldozer clear a passage to the station. The remote location saw operators completely isolated, often for seven or eight months at a time. By the end of the 1920s, however, a road was constructed, providing access from Fame Point to the town of L'Anse-à-Valleau, more than 13 kilometres away.

After years of renewing the Marconi contract, the government finally took over Fame Point in 1957. Other Marconi stations such as Cap-aux-Meules, Battle Harbour and North Sydney also saw their commercial contracts terminated. The Fame Point station was moved to the newly built Department of Transport marine radio station at Rivière-au-Renard, more than 18 kilometres from its historic original site, thus ending the first commercial station of the North American mainland's 53 consecutive years of operation. Like Fame Point, Rivière-au-Renard is also part of the first landfall for shipping coming into the Gulf of St. Lawrence, and lies between the iron-ore centre of Sept-Îles and the Atlantic ports—undoubtedly a good site.

In 1943, the Royal Canadian Air Force (RCAF) placed an order with the National Research Council for seven microwave early-warning systems. German submarines were making their way into the Gulf and Canada needed to fight technology with technology. The early-warning systems were installed at Rivière-au-Renard, Québec; Cape Ray, Newfoundland; St. Paul Island in Cabot Strait; Tofino, British Colombia; Bagotville, Québec; Clinton, Ontario; and Dorval Airport in the greater Montréal region. One of the more useful elements of microwave radar is that the radiation pattern emitted lies close to the surface of water. Small objects such as periscopes or submarines running awash can be detected at greater ranges than most conventional long-range sets could at the time. Without an effective scheme for identifying small, friendly coastal vessels, however, the radar equipment proved useless in the 1943-44 anti-submarine campaign.[12]

The Rivière-au-Renard site still operates to this day from the same location chosen in 1957. The centre also maintains telecommunications sites at Rivière-au-Renard, Cap des Rosiers, Forillon, Carleton, Newport and Heath Point, Québec.

Grosse-Île

The numerous applications for wireless did not go unobserved by Prime Minister Laurier and his government. The Department of Marine and Fisheries sought Marconi's expertise in 1904, when three government ships—the *Stanley*, the *Canada* and the *Minto*—were outfitted with wireless stations. Ship owners of the day felt that intercommunication among the St. Lawrence stations would greatly enhance the whole communications system.[13] In the same year, the department increased the maximum output of the St. Lawrence stations, giving each an effective communication range of 415 kilometres. By 1906, the number of wireless stations in eastern Canada reached 13. The additional Marconi stations were at Camperdown and Sable Island, Nova Scotia; Point Riche, Newfoundland; Pointe-au-Maurier and Grosse-Île, Québec; and Cape Bear, Prince Edward Island—all sites that could conceivably have been

---

[12] *The War History of the Radio Branch*, National Research Council of Canada, Radio Branch (Ottawa: Report no. ERA-141, unclassified, 1948), p. 102.

[13] O.G.V Spain, Commander, Canadian Marine Service, *Department of Marine and Fisheries Report* (Ottawa: December 12, 1904).

chosen for their picturesque settings alone. Most of the stations are located on high perches.

Grosse-Île already had a colourful past—albeit an unfortunate one—before the Marconi station was built. Since the early 19th century, the island had housed a quarantine station for new immigrants and now quietly harboured the mass graves of 12,000 individuals, mostly from Ireland, who had succumbed to a plague, several epidemics and other illnesses. Now, it was home to both a quarantine station and a Marconi wireless station.

The Grosse-Île site established another link in the chain of wireless stations stretching from the Great Lakes to Newfoundland's Belle Isle and Cape Race. After 15 years of operation, however, the Grosse-Île wireless station, call sign VCD, was declared redundant and, in 1927, it and the quarantine station were closed. The quarantine station moved to Québec City and the city's already-existing wireless station took over where the Grosse-Île site left off. Cyprien Ferland, later a supervisor for Marconi Wireless of Canada, began working at VCD in 1916. It was his first job as a wireless operator.

Pointe-au-Père and the *Empress of Ireland*

"The adventures and hardships of a wireless telegrapher's life more than half a century ago can easily be described but is seldom understood by those who followed us after the 1930s—even less by the present and future generation of operators," said Cyprien Ferland who later worked at the Pointe-au-Père station. Pointe-au-Père's call sign, VCF, is that of today's Mont-Joli MCTS centre. This remote station was indeed forged by the pioneers who first came to the site in 1907.

At the turn of the century, Pointe-au-Père was a town of some 1,000 people. The south-shore town lay open to the St. Lawrence River, and houses stood along what was then called King's Road. The Pointe-au-Père station was founded to establish a vital link in the network of stations that provided St. Lawrence steamers with weather conditions from the Great Lakes to Labrador. The Pointe-au-Père site also eased the work of river pilots as the ships could report their arrival ahead of time, significantly reducing boarding and disembarking times.

The Pointe-au-Père station was part of the second wave of wireless stations constructed in the Laurentian region—at Québec City, Grosse-Île, Belle Isle and Port Menier on Anticosti Island. A turn-of-the-century operator at Pointe-au-Père earned $35 a month for seven-day weeks. Later, the urgency of World War I reduced the staff of most coastal stations to just two men, who together stood 24-hour continuous watches. In their off-duty time, operators maintained the station where regular upkeep requirements ranged from painting the 55-metre mast to prepping the gasoline engine and all parts of the equipment—the dynamo, exciter, alternators, condensers and transformers.

Pointe-au-Père gained notoriety during the tragic marine disaster involving the *Empress of Ireland* in 1914, one of the worst maritime tragedies in history, second only to the sinking of the *Titanic*. The *Empress of Ireland* sank after it collided with the Norwegian collier *Storstad* off the coast of Rimouski. Of the 1,477 passengers and crew, only 465 survived. The ship's distress signals were picked up at VCF, and operators there notified the pilot boat *Eureka* and the small mail-boat, *Lady Evelyn*, which responded to the call for assistance.

Decades later, in 1980, Captain Jacques-Yves Cousteau, at the helm of the *Calypso*, headed an expedition along the St. Lawrence River/Great Lakes System. At the very beginning of their journey, Cousteau and his crew located the *Empress* off the shore of Rimouski. Upon announcing his discovery, Cousteau welcomed a passenger aboard the *Calypso*. Ronald Fergursson, the last wireless operator of the *Empress of Ireland*, recalled his experience when the ship sank. He said he had had barely enough time to recover from the shock and trauma of the accident when he was rushed back to work—in the Marconi office on board the rescuing ship, *Lady Evelyn*. On the *Evelyn*, the exhausted and shaken operator found that no paper was available to copy messages. Toilet paper had to do.

Antonin Blouin, an operator at Grosse-Île, received and copied the *Empress of Ireland*'s distress signal. Blouin later became the first Canadian to teach Morse code and meteorology. He opened his school on William Street in Montréal. The opening coincided with the outbreak of World War I, which created a pressing need for radio operators. The new recruits, because of the importance and urgency of their work, were given on-the-job training. Before Blouin's foray into teaching, it was Marconi who sent instructors to Canada.

Because Pointe-au-Père was a Marconi station, it eventually suffered the fate of all privately run stations. In 1960, Pointe-au-Père was moved to Mont-Joli, Québec, part of a government bid to centralize all marine-communications services. Standardizing equipment and operations was a top priority. Operators and technicians came under Air Services, whose reign over marine Telecommunications & Electronics (T&E) lasted until 1978. Incidentally, Mont-Joli was commissioned as an international air-to-ground communications station along with another station at Resolute, Northwest

Territories. Both provided service to polar flights between Europe and the west coast of North America.

A separate T&E branch opened in 1974 to better serve the needs of the Canadian Coast Guard at a time of increasing marine services. The Mont-Joli Coast Guard Radio station was formed at this time; it left its airport site in 1989 for the Royal Bank building on Jacques Cartier Street in Mont-Joli. On March 27, 1997, the services of Mont-Joli Coast Guard Radio were integrated at Les Escoumins, Québec. The station closed its operations after approximately 90 years of service.

Back in the 1950s, in peaceful Gaspé, an incident occurred that illustrates Cyprien's earlier statement concerning the adventures and hardships of a wireless telegrapher's life. Because English has long been the language of shipping, French-speaking operators in Québec and elsewhere were encouraged to learn English. For his part, Charles Dufresne, once officer in charge at Rivière-au-Renard, learned English and signalling in the Royal Canadian Navy. And because of their first-hand knowledge of particular incidents or problems, some operators accompanied village doctors to quarantined or distressed vessels in the Gulf of St. Lawrence. It was indeed a far cry from normal, daily duties.[14] Dufresne often agreed to step away from his daily duties to work with the village doctor either as an interpreter or to provide assistance. No adventure was too perilous for Dufresne, a character trait shared by many mariners.

One day, both doctor and operator boarded a trawler headed for a distressed vessel heaving in the Gaspé Passage. Dufresne had earlier been radioed that two passengers were seriously ill and that medical assistance was urgently needed.

Conditions in the Gaspé Passage were good that day. The doctor and Dufresne discussed ordinary town matters while en route. The distressed vessel came into view and the trawler slowed its pace. The Gaspé natives boarded the vessel as the two boats lingered hull to hull. Dufresne translated the initial contact with the ship's crew and the vessel's first officer quickly led the way to the ailing men. As they opened the door to the sick men's quarters, the doctor and Dufresne found one man battling to stay alive and another lying dead in his bunk. They had arrived too late. Left unattended for just a few minutes, one of the men had died. For Dufresne, the incident reinforced his tie with the sea, with those it has claimed and with those he would not let it claim.

---

[14] Today the practice of tending to the sick, or anything that falls under the category of emergency, is handled by Search and Rescue units of the Canadian Coast Guard.

Cap-aux-Meules Coast Guard Radio

Further downstream from the Gaspé Passage, in the Gulf of St. Lawrence, lie the Magdalen Islands. A Marconi radio station was built there in 1911. It was from this station that the much-vaunted "voice of the gulf" was heard. For many years, Coast Guard vessels knew well the voice of Jean-Paul Desaulniers, a long-time operator at Cap-aux-Meules Coast Guard Radio, call sign VCN, as the ghost of the gulf. Because of exceptional propagation conditions, Desaulniers' voice could be heard further than most stations covering the adjacent areas.

In 1983, after innumerable renovations, the site was closed in favour of a new building, half a kilometre down the hill from the original Marconi site, in the harbour of Cap-aux-Meules. To this day, however, the original location still houses receiving and transmitting equipment.

Today's communications are a long way from yesterday's marine radio. As in other fields, technology becomes increasingly automated, replacing workers. Remotely controlled sites are the new trend because they are significantly less expensive to operate. But there is also a hidden cost. The Cap-aux-Meules MCTS centre, for example, is the focal point of the local fishing community. Operators say that they know the local area and that "remote" service would not be as good, even if Rivière-au-Renard took over. Area fishermen believe that they would lose a vital, local communications link and seem unable to reconcile that Cap-aux-Meules might ever close. "Who better to know the precise location of buoys [markers that help find distressed vessels] than a Cap-aux-Meules operator?" they ask. Rivière-au-Renard personnel would never be as entrenched in the community as the local operators, claim some residents. Unfortunately for the community and local operators, the "remoting" of Cap-aux-Meules' service to Rivière-au-Renard was carried out on April 21, 1998.

Sept-Îles

While the local presence of marine radio stations is waning into insignificance,[15] some such as Sept-Îles remain on the air.

In 1905, a station opened at Clark City, near Sept-Îles, Québec. At the time, the Marconi employees were considered outsiders in Clark City

---

15 The situation is similar in other countries. In Sweden, for example, the 85-year-old Göteborg Radio station, call sign SAG, closed in January, 1995. The legacy of these stations, however, is full testament to the invaluable assistance they gave to mariners across the globe.

as everyone else worked for the Pulp and Paper Company—the only local sign of civilization at the time. The operators became greatly dependent on the company and vice versa.

Clark City, call sign VCK, handled a good deal of ship traffic, but its primary role was to work as a relay, or point-to-point, station with the south-shore stations of Fame Point and Pointe-au-Père. VCK competed with the Canadian National Telegraph for the north-shore commercial traffic and, for this reason, was busy with night-letter traffic[16] between midnight and 5:00 a.m.

The Marconi station at Clark City reached its peak of activity at the time of the first transatlantic flight in 1922 by Captain Fitzmaurice. The captain was forced to land his plane at nearby Greenley Island after running out of gas. The next three days at VCK were devoted almost exclusively to dispatching press statements.

Improvements in communication coverage at other sites, however, eventually rendered VCK redundant and the station was closed in the mid-1920s. But by the early 1950s, ship movements had increased dramatically on the St. Lawrence. To serve the increasing vessel traffic in the specific area of Sept-Îles, the service at the existing aeradio station was expanded by adding a coast station facility, and a new marine radio beacon was constructed on Carrousel Island, adjacent to the port at Sept-Îles. VCK was active again; the year was 1954. The Coast Guard Sept-Îles marine radio station was moved from the airport to its present location on Brochu Street in 1976.

Sept-Îles Coast Guard Radio maintains a relay at Harrington Harbour, the site of another original Marconi station. The Harrington Harbour station, call sign VCJ, was poorly equipped and only operated when the Strait of Belle Isle ship traffic was flowing. VCJ closed in 1921 after only about 15 years of service.

Operators were an integral and worthy part of the great whole that was the wireless network. But there were times when they were not overwhelmingly appreciated. For instance, one day Sept-Îles Coast Guard operator George Gadbois received a position report from a vessel plying the St. Lawrence. The coordinates were unfamiliar to Gadbois. He went to a nearby map to verify the ship's position, returned to his key and tapped out:

---

[16] Night-letter traffic involved commercial messages transmitted from wireless networks to the landline networks. These messages were processed at night because of lower priority. Given the profitability of this type of traffic, operators working the graveyard shift could increase their income significantly.

"How many deer do you see?"
"What?" was the reply.
"How many deer do you see?" asked Gadbois again.
"Why the question?" the ship operator asked.
"The QTH [position] you gave puts you smack dab in the middle of Anticosti Island. How many deer do you see?"

Anticosti Island is a wildlife sanctuary with a dense deer population. Anticosti Island locals are even affectionately referred to as *chevreuils* (deer). Needless to say, the ship operator did not find the incident amusing and was eager to sail out of Sept-Îles Coast Guard Radio's range of coverage.

Rivière-du-Loup

Rivière-du-Loup marine radio was of particular benefit in the stretch of the St. Lawrence between Île d'Orléans and the Saguenay River, where the topography of the north shore made communication with Québec marine radio difficult and, at times, impossible. A new marine radio station at Rivière-du-Loup, Québec, began serving the shipping traffic on April 1, 1965. The new station was slated to use the call sign VCD, the same one the Grosse-Île station had used at the beginning of the century.

The station's operations centre and receiving facilities were located a little less than five kilometres from downtown Rivière-du-Loup, from where the station's transmitters were remotely controlled. The equipment was the latest in Canadian design and manufacture, providing ships the best possible radio service.

The station operated on a daily basis year-round, providing a message service to ships on radiotelegraphy frequency 415-490 kHz and on radiotelephony (MF and VHF). A marine telephone service eventually became available on MF and VHF channels 26, 57, 59 and 81. The station closed in May, 1980, with its operations consolidated at other sites.

Chapter 2

Newfoundland and the Titanic

When anyone asks me how I can best describe my experience in nearly forty years at sea, I merely say, uneventful. Of course there have been winter gales, and storms, fog and the like. But in all my experience, I have never been in any accident. . .or any sort worth speaking about. I have seen but one vessel in distress in all my years at sea. I never saw a wreck and never have been wrecked nor was I ever in any predicament that threatened to end in disaster of any sort.

E.J. Smith, 1907
Captain, R.M.S. Titanic

The dramatic irony now evident in Captain Smith's statement adds further meshing to the entrapping tale of the *Titanic*. When the unimaginable really happened, people were astounded. They found it inconceivable. The superliner had sunk!

The *Titanic* went down on a freezing morning in the mid-Atlantic at 2:30, April 15, 1912. The *Titanic*, call sign MGY, struck an iceberg 600 kilometres off the coast of Newfoundland, in a region later known as Iceberg Alley, around 11:30 p.m., April 14. It is the world's greatest recorded maritime tragedy ever, claiming more lives than any other. The majestic ship, invoking at once class distinction, human error and bravery, still grips people with its wonder and horror. Tragedy often results in belated change. The *Titanic* disaster spurred a redrafting of international marine communications regulations.

Shortly after hitting the iceberg, Captain Edward J. Smith, a distinguished gentleman who had spent his life at sea, assessed the extent of the damage with his officers. He estimated the ship would go down in two and a half hours. The *Titanic* furnished 1,178 lifeboat spaces for the 2,227 people on its maiden voyage. The superliner was approximately 160 kilometres south of Newfoundland's Grand Banks. The sea, at 31 degrees Fahrenheit, quickly flooded the bow compartment. The

Titanic listed five degrees to starboard and was going down by the head. The ocean floor lay four kilometres down.

Passengers had already retired to their cabins when some may have wondered what the small jolt had been. The iceberg made a 90-metre gash in the ship's hull below the waterline, beginning at the bow and running along the starboard side.[17] The rupture enabled flooding into the forward six water-tight compartments. The *Titanic* was designed to survive the flooding of three compartments, maybe four depending on which ones filled up.

The *Titanic* carried two radio operators; most other vessels had just one. The superliner's radio room, or Marconi office as it was commonly called, was on the forward port side of the boat deck. The equipment covered one side of the Marconi office and the sleeping quarters took up the rest of the restricted space. The equipment consisted of a rotary disk charger fed by a five-kilowatt generator powered by the ship's 110-VDC system. The *Titanic*'s receiver was a magnetic detector activated by a clockwork mechanism with a hand crank, and was connected to the Marconi tuner circuits. The possible wavelength coverage was between 300 and 2,500 metres. In good conditions MGY could communicate up to 3,300 kilometres, making this wireless equipment the most powerful afloat.[18]

The senior operator was Jack Phillips who, incidentally, had celebrated his 25th birthday the day before the accident. Phillips had graduated from the British Marconi school and sailed on several ships. Harold Bride, also a Marconi graduate, was the second operator. Wireless operators were not yet considered officers on ships. They were seen merely as employees—Marconi employees with whom the crew rarely fraternized. They received $30 a month and each worked 14-hour watches.

On the evening of April 14, 1912, Jack Phillips was at the key. Official traffic had piled up and he was busy sending the backlogged messages to Cape Race, MCE, in Newfoundland. The ship had been without communication for about seven hours, but the operators did fix the equipment before the collision. The messages or Marconigrams included names such as Astor and Guggenheim, people who knew the lure of sending messages through the ether.

---

[17] At the British inquiry in 1912, Edward Wilding, a Harland & Wolff naval architect, proposed that the uneven flooding in the six compartments meant each had suffered unique, continuous damage. His testimony was ignored, and the nature of the damage is still debated today.

[18] E.A. D'Onofrio, "We Heard Them Playing Autumn," *Sparks Journal* (Society of Wireless Pioneers, vol. 4, no. 4, 1982), p. 28.

Because of the atmospheric conditions that evening, the *Titanic* lost contact with Cape Race, and Phillips had to wait until the "skip" improved. The work was trying, especially with the cacophony of static and interference (QRM[19]) from other stations in the operator's eardrums. Phillips received several iceberg reports and passed them on to the bridge. One report in particular came from the *Mesaba,* which warned of pack ice and icebergs in the area of 42° to 42° 25' N   49° to 50°30' W. The *Mesaba* message never reached the bridge. Phillips plopped a paperweight on the report with the intention of relaying it to the bridge after he finished with Cape Race. The workload was overwhelming and both operators were exhausted. When the *Californian* interrupted Phillips with more iceberg reports, the *Titanic* operator fired back, "Shut up, shut up, I'm busy with Cape Race." Phillips apologized to the Cape Race operator and asked for a repeat.

The wireless operator of the *Californian,* Cyril Evans, thought the rebuff unnecessary and heavy-handed, although he would have normally waited for communications between the *Titanic* and Cape Race to end before interjecting. Evans had had a long watch and, irritated by the *Titanic's* reply, he closed down for the night. Wireless operators did not necessarily keep continuous watch with their apparatus live. Evans sank into his bunk and went to sleep with an iceberg report unsent. Because of pack ice in the area, the *Californian* was standing at a halt.

The *Titanic* was within sight of the *Californian* and cutting the water at 22.5 knots. Two hours before his watch was due to begin, Harold Bride awoke from his sleep and pulled open the green curtain that separated the bunks from the *Titanic* radio room. He saw the senior operator, Phillips, still busy pounding the key. Phillips informed Bride that the ship had bumped into something and that, if necessary, they would return to Belfast.

Although five iceberg reports had been delivered to the bridge that day, the last report from the *Mesaba* still rested under the paperweight. The operators were bouncing around ideas about the ship's situation when, suddenly, the door opened and Captain Smith himself exclaimed, "We've struck an iceberg. Stand by to send an emergency call, but not before I say so." Smith later returned with the exact location of the liner scribbled on a piece of paper. He asked that the operator send a call for assistance. Phillips promptly responded. He repeated the message six times followed by the *Titanic's* call sign, MGY.

---

[19] QRM is a signal that operators use to indicate interference.

Approximately 160 kilometres away, the *Birma* and other ships in the area were copying "CQD—have struck iceberg—sinking fast—come to our assistance—position latitude 41° 46' N 50°14' W—MGY—." The *Californian*, which was 28 kilometres from the sinking ship, lay dead in the water.

In the meantime, officers on the *Californian* sighted flares on the horizon and reported these sightings to the commanding officer, Captain Stanley Lord, who had retired for the night. "What colour are the flares?" he asked. "White, sir." The captain ordered that they keep a close watch and attempt signalling with the Morse lamp—the wireless operator was not disturbed from his sleep. Strangely, though, the incident was not entered in the ship's official log.

Captain Smith again entered his ship's Marconi office and asked what the exact message was that they were sending. They had been sending the standard CQD call of distress. The younger operator suggested that the newly adopted SOS, which was much clearer, would be easier for any beginner to recognize. The captain replied, "Use it." As Jack Phillips was pounding the brass with the new distress call, little did he know (or likely care) that his frantic actions marked the first use of the SOS call. "MGY CQD CQD SOS SOS CQD—come at once—we have struck an iceberg CQD SOS MGY." Then came the responses. The first came from the *Frankfurt*, then the *Olympic* (the *Titanic*'s sister ship), the *Birma*, the *Mount Temple* and finally the *Virginian*. All were too far away to provide immediate assistance. Then came a quick acknowledgement from the *Carpathia*, which was eastbound for Europe. Wireless operator, Harold Cottam, who was off duty at the time, just happened to be listening in. He heard the good "fist" of Jack Phillips sending 15 to 16 words per minute. "Come at once—we have struck an iceberg—it is a CQD SOS OM—position 41.46 north 50.14 west—MGY." Cottam alerted his sleeping captain, Arthur Rostron, to the news of the sinking passenger vessel. With the captain's urgent response in hand, Cottam raced back to his wireless room and sent a message that the *Carpathia* was 96 kilometres away and coming full speed to assist. The estimated time of arrival was 4:00 a.m. Captain Rostron rallied his officers and crew aboard the *Carpathia* to prepare for the harrowing task that awaited them. The *Carpathia*'s top speed, formerly established at 15 knots, gradually climbed to 17.

Captain Smith was relieved that help was on its way but it was too little, too late. According to his estimates, the *Titanic* would be gone at 2:30 a.m. In the meantime, Cape Race copied the ship's distress call and immediately relayed news of the event to other agencies; most Marconi stations had a telegraph connection, as did most newspapers. Walter Gray, Cape Race's officer in charge at the time of the disaster, had his hands full. The news quickly spread around the globe. Some doubted the news. Could the unsinkable ship really sink?

The crew of the *Titanic* launched the lifeboats as the men in the Marconi office persistently hammered out a very clear SOS. The ship was quickly going down head first, its stern lifting clear out of the water. Some could not—or would not—get into the lifeboats and instead directed themselves towards the drier, sloping areas of the stern. The cold and menacing sea soon became their final fate. According to stories, the house band aboard the *Titanic* was still playing as the ship slipped beneath the cold surface of the North Atlantic.

Power waned and water rushed into the radio room, washing up to the operators' ankles. The captain finally appeared in the doorway and above the sirens, alarms and strident cries of the ailing ship, he bellowed, "You two lads look after yourselves. I release you from your duty." Both men wished each other good luck and made it to lifeboats. Phillips found himself on an upturned craft in the company of the second officer, in whom he later confided the truth about the *Mesaba* iceberg report, the one that never reached the bridge.

Eleven ships steamed towards the *Titanic*. The *Carpathia* was closest at just 33 kilometres away; the *Californian* remained still in the water. Alerted by the flares, the second officer aboard the *Californian* tried to gain his captain's attention, but to no avail. The officer then roused the wireless operator to listen in and to find out more about the situation in the distance. With news of the incident in hand, the officer proved successful in gaining the captain's attention. The *Californian* immediately set course for the stricken ship but it was the *Carpathia* that rescued the *Titanic* survivors.

Operator Phillips slipped into unconsciousness after being rescued and died shortly thereafter. Junior operator Bride was also weak and was rushed to sickbay aboard the *Carpathia*. The *Carpathia* was to rescue many, and the world anxiously awaited news. The lingering question burned in many minds: who had survived? At 8:50 a.m., the *Carpathia* set a course for New York. The *Carpathia's* operator, Cottam, was swamped with calls. So many, in fact, that Bride was brought to the wireless room from sickbay to assist Cottam.[20]

And what of the much-maligned iceberg, whose role in the disaster lasted less than a minute? Most of the icebergs from Greenland, as this

---

20   The *Titanic* account is based in part on an article by E.A. D'Onofrio which appeared in *Sparks Journal* (Society of Wireless Pioneers, vol. 4, no. 4, 1982).

infamous berg was suspected to be, are caught up in the Gulf Stream long before they reach the tail of the Grand Banks and drift north-east until they melt away. But in 1912, the eddies of the Gulf Stream took the bergs south instead, on unusual courses toward Bermuda and the Azores.[21] Even today, Canadian Coast Guard personnel rarely see icebergs travel so far south.

The disaster claimed 1,490 lives from the 2,227 passengers and crew. Most of the crew was lost, including Captain Smith. In the wake of such a tragedy, the international maritime community acted quickly to amend existing conventions. The sinking of the *Titanic* changed maritime history.

London Radiotelegraph Conference

Changes to wireless telegraphy procedures were imminent—two months after the loss of the *Titanic*, a maritime conference convened. Two previous conferences had been held—in 1903 and 1906, both in Berlin. At the 1906 conference, a protocol had been drawn up but six countries refused to sign. In light of the circumstances surrounding the wreck of the *Titanic*, contesting countries yielded to obligatory intercommunication conventions in 1912. Great Britain, Italy and Japan, which had supported the Marconi Company in its bid to restrict non-Marconi communications, announced their support for an article prescribing intercommunication regardless of the system used. Great Britain reversed its policy because of the *Titanic* disaster and also because of the expiration in 1911 of government contracts with the Marconi Company.

The Berlin Conference also made it mandatory for all radio operators to be licensed. Operators' watch-keeping hours at sea were increased and it became a requirement that larger vessels maintain continuous watch. Smaller ships were fitted with automatic alarms which triggered the sounding of three bells, signalling that a ship in distress was in the area. Because of excellent propagation conditions, however, the ship apparatus was often activated by distress calls originating thousands of kilometres away, rendering the system perhaps too efficient.

Transmitting a designated signal on the distress and calling frequency of 500 kilohertz triggered the small-vessel alarm. The signal consisted of 12 four-second dashes with a one-second pause between each dash. The first four of these dashes triggered the alarm; the eight succeeding signals acted as a fail-safe. The automatic alarm sounded in the operator's bunk, the radio room and on the bridge. For their part, ship and coastal stations

---

21 Richard Brown, *Voyage of the Iceberg* (Toronto: James Lorimer & Co., 1983), p. 138.

terminated communications on 500 kilohertz twice every hour. The silent periods were observed for three minutes at quarter past and quarter to every hour to allow any incoming distress calls. The radiotelephone silent periods were, and still are, observed between the hour and again between the half hour and three minutes past. This distress and calling frequency today is 2,182 kilohertz.

Prior to 1912, the lack of strict regulations caused much confusion. For instance, operators would use the very different Continental and American codes indiscriminately. The Continental code was adopted as the International Radiotelegraph Code in a bid to standardize communications. To this end, call signs were officially allotted to each wireless station, with letters specifying either the country of origin or the country of the ship's registration. Ships at this point were still given three-letter call signs as were shore stations. Canada was assigned the block of call signs beginning with VAA to VGZ. Other countries have varying call signs, but the block QAA-QZZ was reserved for code abbreviations still in use to a limited degree today. Incidentally, the word "radio" was coined to differentiate wireless telegraphy from the land-based telegraphy system.

Safety of Life at Sea (SOLAS) Conference

In 1914, SOLAS conference members called for an international ice-patrol system in the North Atlantic to be administered by the United States. The ice-patrol system still works today and has operated non-stop except during the two world wars. Matters such as ice and weather warnings, navigation in dangerous waters, standards for adequate numbers of lifeboats, ship design and stability and, especially, communications took on added significance following the SOLAS conference. The conference made the installation of radio equipment obligatory on certain ship categories such as ocean vessels carrying 50 or more passengers. These must be equipped with radio equipment having a range of at least 160 kilometres. Ships over a certain tonnage must maintain a continuous watch and carry auxiliary radio equipment for emergency use.

Cape Race, Newfoundland

It was the Cape Race station in Newfoundland that took the *Titanic*'s call. Because of its strategic coverage area, Newfoundland telecommunications have long bridged the Atlantic, with ships being the pillars and radio the gangway. Cape Race Radio, VCE, for instance, was an integral part of the Newfoundland marine radio network. The station opened on November 17, 1904. Tucked away at the south-east tip of Newfoundland,

Cape Race juts out into the frigid North Atlantic. In the early days of magnetic and crystal detector receivers, most westbound vessels plying the Atlantic came within range of the Cape Race station. In fact, W.J. Gray and Herbert Harvey were working with this type of equipment at Cape Race VCE when the *Titanic* called. In the early part of the century, Newfoundland stations almost always heard the calls first. Because ship stations could only communicate within 300 to 500 kilometres, Newfoundland stations such as Cape Race and Belle Isle became big revenue producers. In 1920 alone, Cape Race's total revenue was $82,000.

In the years immediately following the *Titanic* disaster, Cape Race was boosted to a working range of about 800 kilometres. The Canadian government agreed with the Marconi Wireless Telegraph Company of Canada when it stated that the two 48-metre wood antenna masts should be replaced by two 77-metre tubular steel masts. The transition was completed in October, 1914, and the Department of Naval Service's share of the cost amounted to $8,000.[22] The Cape Race station was then able to communicate with vessels plying the southern track between New York and Europe. Increasing the station's power renewed its value as a navigation aid, particularly in view of known ice conditions in that area. Over time, however, geography gave way to technology and, as telecommunications improved, Cape Race lost much of its built-in advantage as a prime site.

In 1930, the Cape Race Marconi station closed its doors. Its services were integrated at the long-standing direction-finding government station, VAZ. The direction-finding service gained some recognition when it guided the *R 34* and other transatlantic flights. A year later though, the operations at VAZ were moved back to Cape Race. The station was eventually closed in 1966.

St. Lawrence and Comfort Cove

It could be said that St. Lawrence Coast Guard Radio, located on the south-west tip of Burin Peninsula overlooking Placentia Bay, took over where Cape Race left off the night the *Titanic* sank. The calls to the station on the September day that the *Titanic* was found do not dim the completion of the circle. The calls contributed to radio operator Dennis Pike's satisfaction in completing the circle as he sat at the console, responding much like the Cape Race operator almost 80 years earlier. Just as the loss of the *Titanic* was front-page news around the world, so too was its discovery in 1985. On September 1, 1985, St. Lawrence Coast

---

22 Department of Naval Service, Annual Report, 1915, p. 135.

Guard Radio was inundated following the news that the *Titanic* had been found. The station was hounded by the media, scouts and financiers seeking to learn more about the ship's location. Aboard the *Knorr*, and on subsequent vessels used for various *Titanic* expeditions, crew members' outside conversations were censored. Navy personnel stood watch during all radio and phone conversations. Bottom line: the *Titanic*'s precise location was privileged information.

The expedition to locate the liner was headed by Dr. Robert Ballard, Senior Scientist in the Department of Applied Physics and Engineering at the Woods Hole Oceanographic Institution in Massachusetts and assisted by Jean-Louis Michel of the *Institut Français de Recherche pour l'Exploration de la Mer* (IFREMER).[23] The *Knorr*, Ballard's ship, called the St. Lawrence station with the news that put an end to the 12-year search for the *Titanic*. Ballard's subsequent recommendations led the United Nations to adopt a provision declaring the wreck an international heritage site. And so it is, almost 80 years later, that the *Titanic* and its passengers are finally at rest. But Ballard's historic discovery also led to a reappraisal of the evidence relating to the SS *Californian*. Knowledge of the White Star Liner's precise location "... led to further pressure for the inquiry to be re-opened..."[24]

The 1992 reappraisal adheres closely to the findings of the 1912 inquiry. The distance between the two ships, however, is more than doubled in the 1992 report, but the report clearly states that Captain Stanley Lord of the *Californian* could have bridged the distance separating the *Californian* and the sinking *Titanic*. It is somewhat ironic that the Leyland Line, owner of the *Californian*, was controlled by the same conglomerate, International Mercantile Marine Company, that controlled the White Star Line. Without operator Evans at his wireless station and with just the few white flares fired in the sky, there was no knowing. The 1992 report concludes: "It is for others if they wish to go further into speculation; it is hoped that they will do so rationally and with some regard to the simple fact that there are no villains in this story, just human beings with human characteristics."[25]

Although Captain Lord later found employment elsewhere, he worked for the rest of his life to clear his name. He was unsuccessful. The *Carpathia*—the only boat to rescue passengers during the night of

---

[23] Ballard is also head of the Jason Project, a foundation for distance education that brings interactive learning to schools and homes around the world.

[24] MAIB (Marine Accident Investigation Branch), "*RMS Titanic* Reappraisal of Evidence Relating to *SS Californian*" (England: Department of Transport, March 12, 1992), p. 2.

[25] Ibid., p. 19.

April 15—was torpedoed toward the close of World War I. The passengers in lifeboats that did survive the wreck of the *Titanic* surely would not have made it without the help of Marconi's wireless network. Incidentally, though, Marconi never found out that his fellow countrymen aboard the *Titanic*, the kitchen staff, were denied the opportunity to save themselves. Charles Pellegrino, author of *Her Name, Titanic*, writes "owing to British suspicion and animosity toward Italy, they [Italian kitchen staff] were ushered to their quarters on E Deck aft and locked in."[26]

Contrary to some stations, St. Lawrence and Comfort Cove did not have a long history. In 1965, the Department of Transport began construction of marine radio stations at Comfort Cove and St. Lawrence to replace the older Twillingate and Burin installations respectively. More to the north, the Comfort Cove marine radio station opened in 1967, first airing in January of that year. Its final broadcast went out April 29, 1996. The station's services are now integrated with the St. Anthony station.

The St. Lawrence station initially operated from Burin, Newfoundland. It was moved to the St. Lawrence site in 1966, a year after the marine radio station at Cape Race closed, and after a remarkable history. The services of both Burin and Cape Race were eventually combined to form part of the Decca Navigator chain[27] set up at St. Lawrence. Coincidentally, St. Lawrence, VCP, sent its last broadcast April 14, 1997, a day before the 85th anniversary of the sinking of the *Titanic*. Services previously offered at St. Lawrence were consolidated at the Placentia MCTS centre.

St. Anthony

Gaps in the wireless telegraphy network serving the North Atlantic were soon filled by Marconi stations. By 1910, Eastern Canada formed the hub of Imperial communications in the western Atlantic. Undersea cables came ashore in Nova Scotia, where they connected with a continental system of landlines. The Canadian government's east-coast wireless system, including the stations in the colony of Newfoundland, provided an indispensable link with ships at sea. Today's St. Anthony MCTS centre has evolved from one of Newfoundland's early wireless stations—Belle Isle.

---

26 Charles Pellegrino, *Her Name, Titanic* (New York: Avon Books, 1988), p. 171.
27 In 1946, came the Decca Navigator, a radio positioning system that operates automatically and continuously with groups of land stations. The system works with a pre-mapped grid of lines based on phase-comparison of radio transmissions from a chain of Decca navigating stations. The system operates on a higher frequency than Loran, which was to replace the Decca chain because of its longer range coverage. See Chapter 7 for more on Loran.

Belle Isle had been one of two stations opened by Marconi before his historic transatlantic reception. Superintendent of Government Telegraphs at the time, D.H. Keeley, signed an agreement with Marconi to establish two stations in the Belle Isle Strait—one at Chateau Bay, as the end of the mainland landline, and the other on Belle Isle, 48 kilometres away. The idea to construct the stations was born when the submarine cable between the mainland and Newfoundland proved unreliable due to frequent interruptions caused by iceberg damage.[28]

In his reports of November, 1901, Keeley naively states: "The Chateau Bay station was in readiness on Sunday the 20th of October, when signals from Chateau Bay were received at Belle Isle. None were being received at Chateau Bay." The problem stemmed from defective coherers. The station was deemed operational a short time later, on the 25th. It did not, however, successfully communicate with ships until much later. Even with the limited success of 1901, wireless telegraphy demonstrated its usefulness in replacing wireline telegraphy.

In the busy days of transoceanic voyages, Empress Liner operators plying the Strait of Belle Isle would sometimes send fresh fruit to the operators at the Belle Isle station. Plastic bags filled with fruit were tightly filled with air and floated to shore. The liner sailed so close to shore that operators often heard the captain detailing the surrounding landscape to passengers over the deck speakers. Many ships making the Atlantic crossing came in contact with Belle Isle first upon arriving at North American shores, often broadcasting messages pertaining to berthing needs, and surreptitiously the libidinous needs of the crew.

Belle Isle was in constant communication with a station at Point Amour, which lay 110 kilometres to the west. The construction of the Point Amour station was completed on August 10, 1904, and the following day the station performed its first communication with an outward-bound steamer. Official testing conducted with government steamers demonstrated an effective range of 190 kilometres, on par with other Newfoundland stations.

The station at Cape Ray was completed on October 7, 1904. Cape Ray took most of the traffic from the Cabot Strait, one of Canada's busiest waterways linking the Great Lakes and the St. Lawrence Seaway to the Atlantic Ocean. With the construction of two stations at Point Riche and Pointe-au-Maurier, and the enlargement of the Heath Point and Cape Ray stations, each of which had an effective range of

---

28 A.H. Fraser, *The Development of Radio In Canada*, speech to the Engineering Institute of Canada, 1930, p.4.

communication of fully 415 kilometres, a chain of communication was established and maintained from Fame Point to Belle Isle and from Fame Point to Cape Ray. These stations worked successfully up to the annual closing of navigation on the St. Lawrence.

The Belle Isle and Point Amour stations proved exceptionally valuable in communicating news and weather conditions to steamers coming through the straits of Belle Isle. Reports of current events were supplied only to those vessels equipped with Marconi stations, however. Up-to-the-minute news and current affairs were much appreciated by passengers. Government officials intent on popularizing St. Lawrence shipping were convinced that such a service would secure a loyal customer base. Sure enough, the next year, passenger traffic was greater than at any time in the Dominion's history.

In October, 1970, the Belle Isle station was closed and its services were moved to a new Department of Transport station on Goose Cove Road, some two kilometres from St. Anthony. Unlike many stations, St. Anthony was not moved to the local airport to operate as a combined marine and air services station. In July, 1996, the station moved from Goose Cove Road to its present location in the town of St. Anthony.

The big change signalled by the move from the original Marconi site to St. Anthony was, of course, the streamlining with all land communications networks enabling operators to communicate via telex, and later fax. The disappearance of the Morse code of late is also an emotional situation for some, but its official use has yet to be completely phased out. St. Anthony has taken over all Morse code communications in continuous wave (CW) and is now the only Coast Guard station still to offer the service on the east coast of Newfoundland. The Labrador and Stephenville centres also offer the service. In 1999, however, all official Morse code communications will be completely phased out the world over.

St. John's

In a way, as with the St. Lawrence station, so too did St. John's take over where Cape Race left off. For most of its history, Cape Race had been the point of first contact for ships at sea. St. John's now fills that role. It did not provide the direction-finding services previously offered at Cape Race, but it did maintain long-distance CW communications on MF[29].

---

29   Continuous Wave and Medium Frequency.

In 1951, the Canadian Marconi Company was licensed to operate a public commercial station using the transmitting equipment at Drummondville, Québec, and the receiving equipment at Yamachiche, Québec. The plan was to communicate with a similar station in St. John's, Newfoundland. A link between the mainland and the ex-British colony-cum-Canadian province was a reality. In 1964, marine communications projects included transmitter and receiver sites at St. John's, as well as the rehabilitation of the marine station at Cartwright, Labrador, VOK.

St. John's Coast Guard Radio Service (CGRS) was the eventual product of the Marconi station opened at Signal Hill at the turn of the century. The Marconi Signal Hill station became the Department of Transport's property in 1957. A few years later, on August 4, 1960, the operations at the Signal Hill station moved to Torbay Airport. This was at a time when both air and marine services operated as a single entity under the general rubric Telecommunications & Electronics. Marine communication services were offered from the airport until 1982. St. John's CGRS moved from Torbay Airport in 1982 to settle into its present location on Major's Path. In December, 1997, the station was integrated with the St. John's VTS centre.

Stephenville

The "west coast" station, as it is commonly referred to in Newfoundland, was built in the 1940s. It was located in Corner Brook, Newfoundland, approximately 80 kilometres north-east of the present site in Stephenville. The Corner Brook station used the call sign VOJH. When it moved to Stephenville in 1974 and was combined with air services, it switched to call sign VOJ. In November, 1980, however, a more dedicated marine service was required. As a result, Stephenville Coast Guard Radio, VOJ, was born and established in a reconditioned United States Air Force building on Alabama Drive in the heart of Stephenville.

On July 19, 1990, the station moved again, the third relocation in its 45-year history. With the construction of the Coast Guard base at Port Harmon, all Coast Guard services in Stephenville were combined under one roof. The spacious operations room on the second floor affords an excellent view of the harbour. Its proximity to the harbour also allows more personal contact with users who often visit the station to obtain information on a variety of subjects. Stephenville Coast Guard Radio is now the only bilingual station in Newfoundland and Labrador. Serving the south-west and west coasts of Newfoundland as well as the Gulf of St. Lawrence in Canada's two official languages is an important part of the Stephenville success story.

Stephenville's success also came in another form.[30] On a routine night-shift, an operator at Stephenville came in to work and as usual checked the equipment. MF conditions were better than normal, a situation that can be annoying due to the crashes of static from every thunderstorm within 3,000 kilometres. It was 3:00 a.m., a low point in the shift. Suddenly the operator heard something which sounded disturbingly like a Morse code distress alarm. The operator put on his earphones and turned up the volume. "SOS SOS SOS French fishing vessel 32.27N 27 (static) W." He missed the last of the coordinates. "Bad engine room fire. Abandoning ship. 7 crew members," and then more static.

The operator was quite sure the call came from time zones away. And most probably someone else had picked up the call who was able to get a better position than the Stephenville operator had. But to make certain the call did not go unanswered, the operator passed the message on to St. John's Marine Rescue Sub-centre, which then passed it on to Halifax Rescue Control Centre, and on to an agency in Europe.

Where was the distress? Probably on the other side of the Atlantic, south of the Azores. "Surely someone else got a good position," thought the operator. An hour later, Halifax called Stephenville to confirm the information. An aircraft was departing from the Azores to check it out. At 7:00 a.m. Halifax called back. "Well done. The aircraft searched along the area you gave, and located the seven crew members in a life raft. Two of them were badly burned and a vessel was on the way to pick them up. Oh, by the way, no other station heard the distress call."

---

30 Based on "Just Another Routine Shift," *Contact* (MCTS newsletter, vol. 1, no. 3), p.11-12.

Chapter 3
Calling Nova Scotia

The history of marine radio in Nova Scotia begins with Camperdown Radio, a Marconi station at Portuguese Cove, near Halifax. Construction began at Camperdown on May 4, 1905, and operations started about a month later. To study the useful range of the station, the cable-ship *Mackay-Bennett* was ordered to conduct tests with Camperdown. Joseph Barridon, a trusted Marconi employee, conducted these tests under the supervision of Marconi officer in charge, B.S.Y. Clifton.

While operators were first attempting to communicate with the *Mackay-Bennett*[31], they received the letter V—consisting of three dots and one dash—coming from another ship station. The time was 4:25 p.m., and the ship was Canada's first operational warship, appropriately called the *DGS Canada*. The *DGS Canada* was no doubt sending a repetition of V's for testing purposes. The ship belonged to the Department of Marine and Fisheries, and operated as a small warship, eventually with the Royal Canadian Navy which came into existence on May 4, 1910. It was the *DGS Canada* that carried Canada's first wireless operator. For a long time after, the letter V was used for testing and tuning purposes.

Not unlike Camperdown's first operators, pioneer wireless operators most often began working as landline telegraphists. They brought to wireless their former procedures and practices, including their call codes, two-letter identifiers assigned to each station. Landline telegraphists often used their initials as call signs, demarcating the stations they each manned. In time, however, such unregulated practices disappeared as the wireless network was organized.

Camperdown went on the air with call code "HX" which stood for Halifax. The call sign soon changed to the famous VCS. As with most Canadian stations, Camperdown was equipped on-site for landline

---

[31] Marconi installed the transmitter and receiver in the *Mackay-Bennett* in 1899, when the vessel was sent to New York to report on the famous yacht race between Sir Thomas Lipton's first *Shamrock* and the defending *Columbia*.

telegraphy. Other stations often had a landline telegraph service nearby where messages received via wireless could be retransmitted over wire. Camperdown's initial and only purpose was to forward all messages collected from ships within range of Sable Island and Cape Sable to other agencies, and to receive and process all messages sent by ships able to transmit to the station itself. Powering the coastal station was the usual temperamental gasoline engine, which operators had to start by cranking.

Camperdown also had other variables to deal with—ones that often prevented continuous communications. For instance, static energy often forced stations out of service for several hours at a time. Static still is a problem with some of today's modern equipment and can lead to gradual hearing loss for operators. Compared with today's standards, however, the quality of the receiver greatly limited the capabilities of these stations. Old station logs are marred throughout with "X's" which marked periods of static or natural interference.[32] Over time, however, and with experience, radio operators automatically filter out static. Another popular log entry was the "Bis Tis," signifying that the operator had shut down his noisy gas engine and reverted to a battery for power, greatly reducing transmission capacity.

A few years after the first spark transmitters came into service, studies confirmed that the bursts of energy produced by the sets consisted of electromagnetic waves, within the range of what is known today as the radio frequency band. Not only could these waves be measured, the early wireless engineers discovered, but the spark sets could be designed to transmit and receive on particular waves. This breakthrough set the course for the growth of spark communications technology. The trend was growing, and stations such as Camperdown, Sable Island and Cape Sable began communicating with specific ships, as well as with each other and other stations, on set frequencies. In other words, spark communications technology enabled Camperdown to communicate with Cape Sable while Sable Island communicated with an off-shore vessel, and little interference was generated between the stations.

At the outbreak of World War I, Camperdown was equipped with a new, modern receiver that used a carborundum crystal, and tuned between 200 and 3,000 metres (1,500 and 100 kHz). Years before, on October 25, 1906, Dr. Lee De Forest applied for a patent on the three-element vacuum tube, known as the audion, yet the first receiver fitted with an audion tube did not arrive at Camperdown until 1918, some 12 years later.

---

32   Spurgeon Roscoe's manuscript *Radio Stations Common? Not this Kind.*

Soon, amateur radio operators discovered that the bottom portion of the high-frequency band was of some use for communications. With increasing interference resulting from the ever-growing popularity of communications, official and otherwise, amateurs were forced to work outside of those areas of the spectrum, which at the time were considered the most useful for long-distance communications. International regulators allowed amateur radio enthusiasts wavelengths no longer than 200 metres (1,500 kHz)[33]. Just years before, all frequencies above the present AM broadcast band were considered useless for effective communications; however, as the technology progressed, it soon became evident that all it would take to make use of a wider spectrum of frequencies was a better vacuum tube. It was found that low-power signals on the high-frequency band could cover thousands of kilometers by bouncing them off the ionosphere (an ionized layer of the earth's upper atmosphere). With vacuum tube technology improving, ships began direct communications with their home countries or other stations from anywhere on the globe. This breakthrough in radio technology revolutionized marine communications. One coastal station could work all the message traffic ordinarily handled by a cluster of stations. Consequently, in 1925, the Marconi organization began cutting back on the number of coastal stations, and Camperdown awaited its fate.

The Canadian Marconi Company eventually closed Camperdown in April, 1926, after just 20 years of service, integrating its operations with the nearby Chebucto Head direction-finding station, call sign VAV, constructed in 1917. The buildings that housed the Chebucto facility seemed to be built as temporary structures. Soon after Camperdown was integrated with Chebucto Head, the flimsy architecture was already in bad shape. Various range tests were then conducted at both these sites and the results were clear. Not only were some buildings at Camperdown in better condition, but the Camperdown site itself was definitely a better location for direction finding. In due course, a new radio operations building was constructed at the former Camperdown site in 1934. Camperdown, then, was to provide all the direction-finding and coastal services previously offered at Chebucto Head.

From 1915 to 1922, the Canadian government operated these stations under the authority of the Naval Service. In 1922, however, the service fell back to the Department of Marine and Fisheries. On November 2, 1936,

---

[33] Sharon A. Babaian, *Radio Communication in Canada: An Historical and Technological Survey*, p. 50.

the *Department of Transport Act* was signed, uniting all transportation agencies under the one authority of the new department. With the tenacious C.D. Howe at the helm, the long-established departments of Marine, Railways and Canals and the civil aviation branch of the Department of National Defence were brought together under one roof. In short, all coastal stations became the property of, and were operated by, the Department of Transport—the beginning of a long-standing, although periodically interrupted, ownership. However, this amalgamation at the administrative level changed little of the day-to-day functions at the radio stations.

In Action

By August, 1937, the Department of Transport had 6,543 employees, with an average monthly salary of $85 each. Soon after, the department was called on to make a massive contribution to the war effort.

The outbreak of the hostilities in September, 1939, immediately affected the department's activities. As the war tightened its grip, the department's Merchant Seaman Branch was created to recruit, train and house officers and crew for Canada's wartime Merchant Navy Fleet. Thousands passed through its staffing pools and training schools. By 1945, 200 Canadian-registered merchant ships were staffed by more than 18,000 people recruited and trained by the Branch. The Branch was later able to boast that throughout the war years "no ship ever missed a convoy or failed to sail on time for lack of crew or replacements."[34]

World War II, sometimes called the Electronic War expressly because of the surge in the development and widespread use of communication technology, left its mark on the Camperdown station. Camperdown saw many changes in the early 1940s. One change was the assignment of two operators, rather than one, to each of the three shifts. Another was the termination of all routine communications and broadcasts in order to maintain a continuous distress watch.

By virtue of Camperdown's ideal receiving location, the station actually participated in some wartime action in the Atlantic involving Convoy BX-141 running from Boston to Halifax during the closing months of the war. On January 12, 1945, the minesweeper HMCS *Westmount*, travelling outbound with minesweeper HMCS *Nipigon*, passed the *Boston Gate* vessel. By late afternoon, the *Westmount* had the convoy formed and moving out towards Halifax. Lieutenant R.L.B. Hunter of the Royal Canadian Navy Volunteer Reserve was in command

---

[34] Transport Canada web site.

of both the *Westmount* and the convoy. The two minesweepers were to be assisted with the convoy by Escort Group 27 which at the time consisted of three frigates: the *Meon*, the *Coaticook* and the *Ettrick*.

By definition, a convoy is a system for escorting merchant ships. It can be traced back to the Spanish who, in their colonizing years, transported vast fortunes from the Latin colonies back to Spain. When in a convoy, warships patrol the perimeter of the line of merchant ships, watching for potentially bellicose parties. During World War II, the Royal Canadian Navy was well tuned for this task, regularly escorting ships along the coasts and across the Atlantic. Such an old practice was continued because some of the merchant ships were, themselves, old and could not exceed speeds of 7.5 knots. And maintaining the unity of the convoy requires that no ship exceed the maximum speed of the slowest ship. Convoy BX-141 counted 20 ships, including the *Martin Van Buren*, a recently built vessel owned by the United States government. She joined the convoy loaded with military cargo comprised of provisions, locomotives, vehicles and a regular war-time crew of 41 merchant seamen and a 27-man U.S. naval complement. For their part, the naval ships keeping the patrols and ensuring protection around the convoys had senior officers on board who worked with the convoy Commodore.

Once out of Boston, the two minesweepers kept patrol around the merchant ships. At 2:12 a.m., January 13, 1945, the HMCS *Ettrick* G-27 escort approached and joined the convoy. Later that morning, the *Nipigon* reported to the *Westmount* that her radar was down and could not be repaired. The next evening, the two remaining frigates of Escort Group 27 arrived, and the vessels were scheduled to arrive soon in Halifax. On the morning of January 14, Lieutenant Hunter ordered "cat-gear" to be launched behind the naval escort vessels. "Cat-gear" is an apparatus designed to produce excessive noise at the end of a tow, well away from the stern, to prevent acoustic torpedoes from following the thrashing noise of the ship's propeller. The convoy then broke away from the column formation and proceeded single file. The Escorts of BX-141 were lagging behind because of the noise-creating gear, leaving the merchant ships unprotected.

At this late stage of the war, the German U-boats deployed in this part of the Atlantic were usually type VII's, limited vessels because of their short travel range and their reliance on the larger supply submarines for everything from fuel to relief personnel. German supply submarines such as the U-1232, were type IX C boats, like the one that, under the command of Captain Dobratz, proceeded towards Halifax as the convoy from Boston did the same. Three other such U-boats had been sent out to various positions in the North Atlantic to serve as weather stations. The forecasted weather conditions were transmitted back to German officers who were preparing to pounce on the Allied Forces in the Ardennes Forest in the early part of 1945. This offensive was to be Hitler's last great effort to break the allied offensive whose next move was to cross the Rhine. The U-1232 under Dobratz was armed with acoustic torpedoes, allowing it to simply lie in wait for ships coming into or out of Halifax.

Radio operators on duty in the many radio rooms of the convoy were working routine shifts, unaware of the lurking U-boats. Despite the radio silence between ships, Canadian coastal stations were known to communicate among each other, allowing ship stations to tune in and assuring operators that they were listening to the correct frequency. The communications, even the weather broadcasts, were conducted by secret code.

British Freedom, also a member of the convoy, was proceeding past buoy number one in the swept channel when it happened. Bert Hawling and his two assistants were busy cleaning up the radio room and completing some routine maintenance when she was hit. A torpedo struck the ship's stern. Hawling looked outside through slots in the armour and realized things were worse than he had thought. In no time, the sea was lapping over the after tank tops. Behind the *British Freedom*, the captain of the *Martin Van Buren* immediately gave the order to swing out around the right of the afflicted ship. But Captain Dobratz had just begun. From aboard the *British Freedom*, Hawling witnessed "the ghost," a great white gush of water in the sea—another torpedo launched by U-1232. The *Martin Van Buren* could not brush off the punishing blow. Caught in this great gush of water were four gunners, all but one of whom died. The survivor managed to swim to the starboard raft which had been blown over with him. The HMCS *Comox*, also a member of the convoy, rescued the injured man.

When Captain Martin of the *Athel Viking*, a tanker originally built to carry molasses for the United Molasses Company Limited, saw the two ships being torpedoed, he ordered the ship to manoeuvre alongside *British Freedom*. The *Athel Viking*, like the *Freedom*, took a hit in her stern.

Ed Bloomenthall, an operator aboard the *Martin Van Buren*, was the first to send a distress call. He signalled "SSSS," indicating that the ship had been torpedoed by a submarine. Meanwhile, aboard *British Freedom*, operator Bert Hawling had to revert to the battery supply because the ship's main electrical power was out. A dim light hovered over him as he communicated with VCS. The operators at Camperdown looked at each other knowingly as they plowed through the calls, relaying all necessary requests and recording bearings taken from the direction finder.

Captain Morris of *British Freedom* ordered the crew to abandon ship. Their position was hopeless. Hawling had radioed for a tug, but his efforts were futile. The few remaining crew members felt the ship shudder; the engine room bulkhead had probably yielded to the inflow of water. The bow was rising and soon the funnel would be underwater. Moments later as he sat in a lifeboat, Hawling could see into his cabin which opened aft onto the bridge deck. Some of his personal belongings were falling out the open door, and he looked on as his wicker chair slipped into the oily sea.

One of the four Basset Class Minesweepers, the HMCS *Gaspé*, rescued the crew of *British Freedom*. The HMCS *Gaspé*, however, had hove to clear of the distressed ship and made the lifeboat crew row a good distance because of the 30 depth-charges sitting on the *British Freedom*'s bridge deck. Had these depth-charges exploded while *British Freedom* sank, the force of the blast would have reached the HMCS *Gaspé* even at its cautious distance.

The damage sustained by the *Martin Van Buren* essentially disabled the vessel. The torpedo blew off the rudder, propeller and thrust bearing caps and killed the main engines. The impact of the torpedo explosion caused a five-centimetre crack in the hull that extended well below the waterline. The deck was bulged on the starboard side and cracked on the port side. Because all the watertight bulkheads were leaking, the shaft alley flooded immediately. One of the tugs of the Foundation Fleet was in the area, and the *Foundation Security* took the *Martin Van Buren* in tow just as her fire alarm system went off. A fire was spreading in the five-inch magazine. Flood valves were opened to douse the fire, but it was too late. Captain Hiss gave the order to abandon ship, and the *Martin Van Buren* crew was picked up by the HMCS *Comox*.

Meanwhile, the crew of the *Athel Viking* felt certain that their ship would stay afloat if they could soon get a tow into Halifax. They remained on board and waited. At 3:23 p.m., two crew members sighted a submarine on the surface. The Navy was to later conclude that the sighting had been of a fairmile[35] and not a submarine. The men, however, remained convinced of what they had seen. Camperdown Radio communicated that a tug was on the way. Apparently it never came. Here is what *Athel Viking* crew member, Al Whatley, said about it:

---

35   A Canadian-built ship used extensively in both world wars.

The reason we were not picked up at a similar time as the crews of *British Freedom* and the *Liberty Lightship* [other distressed vessels in the area] is unclear. We stayed aboard for about seven hours until ordered to abandon ship. We were told by VCS that tugs were on the way, but they never arrived. From memory, there were three tugs sent from Halifax but they were all on their way to the *Liberty Ship*. I wouldn't say that we were ignored, but they certainly didn't find us. After seven hours, we had developed a considerable list, causing two lifeboats to swing inboard rendering them useless, and leaving only two boats plus rafts serviceable.

The crew of the *British Freedom* was eventually rescued. Their belated arrival to safety was made possible by the rather crude type 268 radar. Sadly, however, four of the *Athel Viking* crew disappeared and are believed drowned. Captain Dobratz, had surreptitiously got the better of Convoy BX-141.

Radio played many roles during the course of World War II. It was used for communications, as a navigation tool and for detection/intelligence purposes. Radio had also been used in the First World War, but did not truly come into its own as indispensable technology until World War II.

Great strides were made in the technological advancement of radio during the war, especially the development of radio navigation aids. For example, a portable German weather station was set up on the coast of northern Labrador in 1943 to gather crucial weather-related information in the northwest Atlantic. The leading-edge, portable weather station "was a very sophisticated unmanned system that could automatically collect and transmit the temperature, barometric pressure, wind force and direction. A timing device was used to turn on the transmitter . . ."[36] The German system used the high-frequency band, allowing stations in Europe to receive its signals.

Also active at the time were radio-interception operators working in stations such as Point Grey, in Victoria, British Columbia, where operators intercepted the Japanese or KANA code. Many stations existed, in fact, solely to monitor enemy radio traffic. As a result of the ease of access and use of radio by Allied and Axis Forces, each sought to disrupt the enemy's communications by jamming their signals. To this end, equipment such as short-wave direction finders of the cathode-ray type were distinctive because, in addition to their viability in air transport and marine services, their use in interception and monitoring was

---

36 Sharon A. Babaian, *Radio Communication in Canada: An Historical and Technological Survey*, p.71.

exceptionally valuable. The system, however, only came into use at the beginning of 1942.

Radio interference tactics were also employed for offensive purposes. The rapid rate of development and the widespread use of radar-based defence installations, which warned of enemy aircraft, ships or self-propelled bombs in the mid-1940s, spurred the invention and use of specialized radar-jamming devices.[37] With new technology introduced almost daily, by both sides of the war, Dobratz's success in the North Atlantic may have been pure luck.

Transatlantic Communications

On December 15, 1902, a wireless transatlantic telegraphic service was inaugurated between Table Head, Nova Scotia, and Poldhu, England. The following year, on March 28, Marconi introduced a limited press service but it was discontinued because of aerial trouble caused by gales, and Glace Bay, Cape Breton, was selected as a replacement site.

The Marconi Wireless Telegraph Company owned the station. It had been subsidized by Canada in 1902 at a cost of $80,000. With financial backing secured, up went four 64-metre towers, twenty-four 55-metre masts and forty-eight 15-metre masts in May, 1905. In October, 1907, limited commercial operations began with Clifden, Ireland. Some months later, in February, 1908, full commercial service was launched and continued through the fall of 1909. It came to an end, however, in 1909 when the station burned to the ground. The Glace Bay station was rebuilt with a 100-kilowatt DC system replacing the old non-synchronous AC system. The service was simplex[38] and alternate periods were scheduled for transmission and reception.

The receiving station was later transferred to Louisbourg, Nova Scotia, and the transmitter was remotely controlled by Louisbourg operators. In 1921, with the advent of continuous wave (CW) technology, the system of transmission was changed from spark to tube. More changes were made when, the following year, another short-wave CW transmitter was installed for long-distance communications with ships, including weather and bait reports to fishing vessels from the Grand Banks to Newfoundland.

Canada's illustrious standing in transatlantic communication did not end with Glace Bay. The first commercial long-distance beam short-wave

---

[37] Sharon A. Babaian, *Radio Communication in Canada: An Historical and Technological Survey*, p. 72

[38] Simplex worked with one frequency, only allowing one party to communicate at a time.

radio service was established by the Canadian Marconi Company between its station at Drummondville, Québec, and a station at Bodmin, England. Both stations began operations on October 25, 1926. Steady improvements in the methods of wireless communications eventually rendered the Louisbourg station obsolete because it could not compete with the beam service. Soon, hundreds of long-distance short-wave stations operated in practically every country of the world and, as a consequence, international administrators had difficulty fitting them into the already-busy frequency spectrum. A station in Montréal interfering with a station in Toronto was a simple matter to resolve; but a station from the West Indies, for example, interfering with a London station communicating with Montréal could be difficult to rectify.

Before the beam, though, long-wave distance communications were usually carried on long wavelengths of between 8,000 to 20,000 metres. The date October 25, 1926, witnessed a revolution in this phase of radio. Fewer and fewer long-wave stations remained at the end of the 1930s; all new development was in short-wave circuits technology. The Canadian Marconi Company opened the English and Australian short-wave installations in June, 1928. In England the designated frequencies were 18,180 kilohertz for day use and 9,330 kilohertz for night use. The Australian circuit, on the other hand, used the same frequency for both day- and night-time use. At night, signals were shot around the world in the opposite direction to the one they took during the day. Parenthetically, in the mid-1920s, an experimental short-wave voice telephone circuit was activated between Montréal and London, England, which soon developed into viable commercial use.

The Canadian Marconi Company's beam-transmitting station in Canada was at Drummondville, Québec, and its receiving station was at Yamachiche, 42 kilometres north of Drummondville. The stations were linked to the central office in Montréal by landline, and the transmitter was remotely operated from the central office. When an operator in Montréal pressed his key or fed a message tape into a high-speed telegraph instrument, the signals were instantaneously recorded at the distant terminal office, whether 5,000 kilometres away in London, England, or 20,000 kilometres away in Melbourne, Australia.

Incoming signals from the corresponding stations received at Yamachiche were heterodyned to a lower frequency, then amplified and filtered so that they could be conducted on landlines. The landlines consisted of open wire lines and cables. When Montréal received the message, the message was automatically recorded and transcribed for delivery.

The aerial systems at the transmitting and receiving stations were identical. Both were supported on guyed steel lattice masts, with the exact height depending to some extent on the wavelength used. The usual height was about 84 metres with cross arms measuring 27 metres from end to end at the top. The design was characteristic of the short-wave beam system and differed from that previously used at commercial radio stations. At radio stations, the aerial consisted of a series of horizontal wires suspended on a line of masts and connected to the transmitter by a vertical or oblique section. The beam system, on the other hand, consisted of a number of vertical conductors forming a wire curtain suspended from horizontal supporting steel cables attached to the ends of the cross arms. The aerial system was on one side of the masts facing the distant station while the reflector system, similarly constructed, was suspended on the opposite side. For each service, a series of five masts was erected in a straight line and aligned so that the great circle bearing on the distant station was at right angles to the line of the masts.

The usual space between masts was 198 metres, making the total length of each line about 960 metres. The beam left the aerial system at right angles to the plane of the masts and followed the shortest or great circle track in the direction of the corresponding station. This way the beam was received at maximum strength.

Each service used two wavelengths which in turn required two aerial systems, one for day use and one for night use. Interestingly, the England-to-Australia circuit only called for a single wavelength, projecting alternatively in opposite directions. By arranging two similar aerials with one reflector in between, the transmitter could be switched from one to the other easily. In the early testing stages of the circuit, it was discovered that the position and distance of the earth relative to the sun had an effect on the transmission of signals. During the morning, the waves travelled from England to Australia, starting in a westerly direction across the Atlantic and Pacific oceans, following the great circle route which, at 20,000 kilometres, was the longest trajectory. But during the evening, the waves travelled eastward over Europe and Asia, following the shortest route, about 15,000 kilometres.

Each aerial occupied two bays between the masts and consisted of a sheet of parallel elements made up of a number of vertical doublets linked by phasing coils. The aerials were spaced about one-quarter wavelength from a screen composed of twice as many reflector wires. The currents fed into the parallel wires of the aerial were all in phase and under this condition the energy, radiated from each wire, cancelled out in the plane of the wires, but added in the direction at right angles to the plane. The effect of the reflector was to cut off the back radiation from the aerial and to strengthen it in front. As a result, a strong beam of radiation was confined almost to one direction and spread over an angle determined by the dimensions of the aerial. The greatest energy concentration by directional effect for a given area of the aerial and, therefore, for a given cost, was obtained by having equal areas at the transmitter and receiver.

The feeder system was composed of concentric copper tubes, the outer one of which was grounded and the inner tube insulated from it by means of a special porcelain insulator. The feeder system was arranged so that the length of the feeder to each aerial element was exactly the same, ensuring that currents in all aerial wires were in phase.

For its part, the transmitter was specially designed to ensure high-frequency stability, a point of the utmost importance when dealing with short waves. Twenty kilovolts supplied the anodes of tubes in the final amplifier stage, from which ample energy was fed through the feeder system to the aerial.

The receiver was coupled to the reflecting aerial system. A similar feeder arrangement was used as the one at the transmitting station and consisted of nine carefully screened units conveniently mounted on a vertical rack. As the signal passed through the receiver, its frequency in addition to its amplification, was lowered by the heterodyne principle to obtain a suitable value needed for efficient transmission to the central office. Band-pass filters were incorporated in the receiver, allowing certain narrow bands of desired frequencies to pass through. The intensity of the signal finally transferred to the landline was automatically prevented from exceeding a certain maximum value by being passed through a limiting tube which had a suitably biased grid.[39]

Each transmitter had the same circuits as those frequently used in carrier current telegraphy. By superimposing several communication channels on one physical wire circuit, each beam aerial could be efficiently used for simultaneous transmission of telephone or telegraphy messages without any interference between the services. Facsimile transmission could also be used with the beam service, over practically any distance.

---

39   A grid is an electrode in a vacuum tube that controls the flow of current between the filament and the plate. Biassing a grid, in this case, is to negatively charge the currents that flow between the filament and the plate.

The beam system had several advantages over long-wave radio communications. It was cost-efficient, required only a low-energy supply. As well, with radiation restricted to a narrow beam, combined with the screening effect of the reflector at the receiving station and the number of wavebands available, more services could be offered than ever before.

The most apparent advantage of the beam system was that two stations capable of communicating halfway around the world could be built for approximately half a million dollars. The cost of building and laying a permalloy cable uniting New York and the Azores was estimated at $4 million.

The Marconi station acquired by the Royal Navy at Glace Bay, Nova Scotia, in 1937, was soon overloaded by the ever-increasing Navy traffic. Glace Bay was the most powerful station in eastern Canada at the time, and continued to serve the Navy until the end of the war. With the continual expansion of naval activities, there was an urgent need to upgrade communications. To this end, the Royal Canadian Navy acquired its own station, one that was four times more powerful than the Glace Bay station. Halifax Radio, CFH[40], was not only powerful, but was the first Canadian coastal station to use the high-frequency portion of the radio spectrum. Operators could raise this station only on the high-frequency (HF) bands, because CFH did not offer any service on 500 kilohertz and any vessel wishing to communicate with the station had to transmit on HF, a waveband extensively used for long-distance communications.

The transmitters for CFH were located at Newport, Nova Scotia, and the receiving site and operating positions were outside Dartmouth, in the town of Albro Lake. It was the most powerful broadcasting unit in Canada and perhaps the most modern naval radio station in the world. The station had 20 transmitters. The main transmitter had an output of 80,000 watts. A standby diesel power plant ensured uninterrupted service in case of power failure.

The three towers of the main transmitter each measured 170 metres, plus two other towers just over 97 metres each. Each tube in the main transmitter's power amplifier weighed an incredible 113 kilograms. Standing at a height of 5.5 metres, the tubes had to be cooled by forced streams of purified air to sustain the 350,000-volt electrical charges. The main aerial insulators measured more than three metres, and were tested to withstand 40,860 kilograms of force, not to mention the strain of

---

40   During peace time, the call sign was CFH, but during the hostilities the call sign was continually changed.

350,000 volts. Despite the station's final $6-million construction cost, the Royal Canadian Navy estimated that just three months of North Atlantic traffic saw the government recuperate the cost, simply by virtue of the station's efficient handling of the increased shipping. In 1944, CFH averaged one million code groups a month.[41]

At war's end, the Albro Lake station continued its operations and became part of the British Commonwealth communications scheme, the largest marine communications network of its kind. Under this scheme, the world's oceans were divided into several zones. Halifax CFH became the control centre for the western regions of the North Atlantic. A similar station existed in Vancouver, CKN, which controlled the north-eastern Pacific.

As the post-war era began, the stations continued their practice of broadcasting traffic lists. The broadcasts consisted of listing ships in alphabetical order, according to call signs, and consecutively alerting each ship to stand by for messages. After broadcasting the list, messages specific to particular needs were then transmitted. This practice had begun during the war when ships rarely used their transmitters in order to avoid revealing their positions. British Commonwealth stations each had a unique frequency assigned for broadcasting traffic lists. All of the controlling stations used identical working frequencies in each band for direct communication with ships. This meant that an operator calling Halifax Radio CFH, for example, could have Portishead Radio, GKL, in England answer and copy the messages. The Commonwealth method was economical and efficient, since there were no additional charges to forward a message sent from one station to another. Because of this system, a ship could actually sail the world with little trouble, and with nothing more than a medium-frequency (500 kHz) transmitter.

Ships making use of the British Commonwealth stations enjoyed unprecedented convenience, and needed only to contact the closest controlling station to transmit a TR message (a service message stating the ship's position and its next port of call). There were many British Commonwealth stations around the world, with several smaller stations participating as partners in this global communications scheme. For instance, stations in Australia, New Zealand, South Africa, Singapore, Hong Kong, India, Malta, Gibraltar, Jamaica and Bermuda allowed those ships fitted with medium-frequency transmitters to receive their messages through this vast web without additional expense. A ship could send a

---

41 Spurgeon Roscoe's manuscript *Radio Stations Common? Not this Kind.*

message to Sydney, Australia, via Camperdown, for the same charge as sending it direct to Sydney. Since the majority of ships were of British registration, ship owners incurred neither the expense of installing industry-standard stations nor of paying extra charges for messages carried around the globe.

Following the war, however, criticism of the system did arise, mostly in the form of questioning the prudence of imparting ships' destinations and coordinates to coastal stations in no way related to those ships. If a station had a message for a specific ship, critics claimed, would it not be logical to let her operator call in and collect the message instead of wading through other ships' messages to get to her own. Some operators found the whole process imbued with unnecessary chatter. Twenty years passed before the British Commonwealth Scheme was abandoned in the late 1960s in favour of the American system of simply "calling in" for messages.

After the war, Halifax CFH carried on under the same staffing arrangement as it had when it first went on the air in 1943. Charlie Williams was the Department of Transport officer in charge in 1943, and he and the naval telegraphists handled all north-east Atlantic radio traffic except for the passenger liners. The station began handling commercial traffic at 8 a.m., January 1, 1946. The petty officer telegraphist in charge of the watch that day got excited about taking on commercial shipping, and jumped the gun, starting at midnight local time. Department of Transport operators had previously drawn lots to determine who would have the honour of opening the station. Ernie Falvey won the draw and arrived at Halifax CFH at 8 a.m. to find not only the station open eight hours ahead of schedule but the place in a state of complete disarray. Messages were bereft of origins, checks and times; names were inaccurate; call signs were missing or inaccurate and, worst of all, no QRC's (name of the private company handling the accounts) were recorded. Falvey was in for a long day.

Another instance since adopting commercial services saw Ernie Falvey receive the following message from the *Queen Mary*, call sign GBTT: "QTC264" (I have 264 telegrams) "QSG30" (I will send 30 of these at a time). The grand passenger vessel was bound for New York from Europe and when Shirley Booth, another operator at the time, relieved Falvey from duty that same afternoon, the *Queen Mary* twice messaged "HVE PRESSE CK4000", which amounted to a 4,000-word text destined for the *London Telephoto News*. Both operators busily pounded out message text until the stroke of midnight. Also on board the *Queen Mary* were a number of war brides from England, each of whom was allowed to send one telegram courtesy of the British government.

Halifax Radio VBQ

By 1936, radiotelephone technology, another incarnation of wireless technology, had made such significant advances that the Department of Transport installed a station dedicated to this mode of communication to serve ships in the Halifax area. The station was built at Citadel Hill in the city of Halifax, a location it kept only five years before moving in 1941 to the upper floor of the Halifax Post Office building. A signal station for visual communications was mounted on the roof of the Post Office and was operated by the Women's Royal Canadian Naval Service during the last years of the Second World War. Civilian signalmen took over after the war.

The radiotelephone station VBQ was known simply as Halifax. The operators handled radiotelephone duplex calls, which provided direct links between ships and the regular telephone system. Halifax VBQ maintained a continuous radiotelegraph service between Halifax and the radio operators at Sable Island, VCT, and with Ottawa radio, VAA. Another part of the station operators' duties involved supplying an operator for the Sambro Lightship. For many years, VBQ operated with only one transmitter, a Collins AG10, but eventually acquired a second one.

Post-war Camperdown

C.R. Spracklin was officer in charge at Camperdown at the end of World War II. The Navy had turned the relatively new Port War Signal Station over to the Department of Transport, which instituted a series of changes in the two Camperdown stations. By the early 1950s, the signal station housed mess accommodations, the main radar set and a low-power radiotelephone used to communicate with local lighthouses and the Halifax Pilot Boat. The staff of the signal station used the radiotelephone, while the radar was operated by Camperdown VCS. The Camperdown station consisted of the main transmitter, a type LCS5 with a one-kilowatt output, backed up by a Marconi LTT4 for emergencies. A Marconi TM11 was used for ships fitted with radiotelephone equipment. The National Research Council designed type 268 radar and two cathode-ray type direction finders were also installed at the station. One of these direction finders operated on the usual radiotelegraph direction-finding frequencies in the MF CW band, and the other operated on the radiotelephone frequencies of the two-megahertz band. The medium-frequency direction finder could be connected to either Bellini-Tossi loops or to an Adcock Array, while the two-megahertz apparatus had its own set of Adcock aerials.

Since the radar provided only the ships' bearing and range, and the direction finder provided identification and bearing only, the radar and direction finding at Camperdown worked in tandem with the low-power radiotelephone. This method of blending technologies provided the utmost accuracy for determining bearings and precisions. This, in turn, allowed pilot boats and incoming vessels to find each other in low-visibility conditions, and enabled operators to follow a vessel's progress into the harbour.

During the 1940s, radiotelephone communications increased considerably. The large fishing vessels replaced their radiotelegraph equipment with radiotelephone equipment and smaller vessels began installing units at a brisk rate.

The *Italia*

Early one morning in 1952, Ernie Falvey was on radar watch at Camperdown. The type 268 radar, a World War II leftover designed and built by the National Research Council, afforded a mere 6.6-kilometre coverage. Fog had formed in Halifax Harbour, reducing visibility to a 100 metres or so. Camperdown had a large chart mounted on a pedestal beside the type 268 radar, and the operators of the radar watch were required to plot the position of any ship, leaving or entering Halifax— a sequence executed as soon as a ship appeared on the radar screen, and repeated every 15 minutes thereafter.

At 11 a.m. on that shrouded morning, Ernie Falvey placed the Panamanian ship SS *Italia* on the chart. The *Italia* was approaching at 95 degrees and heading for the outer automatic buoy. According to station regulations, Falvey did not have to plot the vessel's position again until 11:15 a.m. Falvey, relaxed in demeanour, got up from his chair and looked out at the gloomy weather as he walked to the operating position where John Weir, the duty operator, sat. As he stood next to Weir, Falvey nonchalantly checked the screen and saw the *Italia* looming large. It jumped out at him. The *Italia* was headed towards the Black Can Shoal buoy. It had probably mistaken the buoy for the outer automatic. The Black Can Shoal buoy is to the north-east of the outer automatic. Above the shoal, there is only 5.5 metres of water and the *Italia* was drawing 9.5 metres. The *Italia*, with 1,500 passengers on board, was headed for disaster.

Falvey did not have to tell Weir twice to call the *Italia*. Although he could have called the *Italia* on 500 kilohertz, Weir grabbed the radiotelephone and contacted the pilot boat instead. The Department of Transport had installed radiotelephone facilities for communicating with vessels of the Pilotage Service at Halifax in 1947. Captain Harris Mosher, Falvey's brother-in-law, was in the pilot boat headed for the *Italia*. It is unclear how either Weir or Falvey got their message through, but the vessel did reverse to full speed astern. The clanging telegraph bells added to the rising panic aboard the *Italia*, the engineers yelling madly at each other while shifting into reverse and pushing the throttles to the limit. The *Italia* escaped tragedy by a wing and a prayer.

Radio Stations Combined

The quick development of radiotelephone, and the fact that in the decade or so after the war many ships were fitted with radiotelephone equipment, left the future of some older stations in doubt. With the closing of the radar and direction-finding services, Halifax VBQ was moved to Camperdown Radio, making it necessary to build a transmitter site at Pennant Point and a remote receiver site just south of Ketch Harbour. On November 1, 1962, the newly combined station was baptized Halifax marine radio VCS. The word "marine" denoted the station's distinction, setting it apart from other radio stations across Canada. A number of aeradio and coast stations were merged under the same roof to slash the costs incurred by running similar stations in the same area. Some operators still maintain that working both the air and marine traffic greatly increased their work load, but nevertheless served to hone their copying skills.

Halifax marine radio was one of the few stations never to be combined with the surrounding local aeradio stations, although some operators did work occasionally at the aeradio station at Halifax International Airport, 64 kilometres away. The west-coast sister of VCS, Vancouver, VAI, worked alongside Vancouver Aeradio at Vancouver International Airport.

In a move to radically cut costs and institute efficient service, the Department of Transport not only amalgamated many of the coast stations, but also decided to open a school to train all new operators above and beyond the training required to get their commercial-class certificates. The Air Services Training School opened its doors on the upper floor of the terminal building at Uplands Airport, Ottawa, in 1960. By 1965, amendments to radio regulations at the Montreux International Telecommunication Convention, logically determined the end of second-class certification requirements for operators at Canadian stations. From 1965 on, operators required a high-school diploma and a certificate obtained from the Air Services Training School to operate either or both Canadian marine and air radio. In 1979, the school moved to more modern accommodations in Cornwall, Ontario.

During the early 1960s, the Royal Canadian Navy equipped most of its vessels with radioteletype, while endorsing the end of operator training in radiotelegraphy. The Royal Canadian Navy also sought, however, to retain radiotelegraphy at CFH for the smaller and auxiliary vessels and as a backup to the regular teletype communications. Consequently, the sector of Halifax CFH referred to as the British Commonwealth Scheme was transferred to VCS in 1964. Further expansion of VCS was required to house the high-frequency transmitters and receivers, and additional operators were needed to work the equipment. Improved shipboard equipment, such as more powerful and compact transmitters and receivers, precipitated the demise of the old scheme. In 1968, the British Commonwealth Scheme was finally and completely phased out.

Because of the amalgamation of Halifax CFH and Halifax Radio VCS with Halifax Radio VBQ at Camperdown, and because of the deteriorating state of the accommodations, the Department of Transport decided to improve the station's building and equipment. For various reasons, these changes would take place at the Camperdown Radio Site in Ketch Harbour. Weighing heavily in favour of this move was the equipment at the receiver and transmitter sites which had to be connected to the operating position at Camperdown via telephone lines leased from Maritime Telegraph and Telephone Company Limited. The Ketch Harbour site eliminated the need for remote receiver lines, and the remote transmitter site at Pennant Point was much closer to Ketch Harbour, cutting down on leasing costs.

It was in March, 1970, that Halifax marine radio VCS, the largest station in Canada, moved from its original site on the hill overlooking the approaches to Halifax Harbour to the more modern operations building in Ketch Harbour. The Camperdown site was no longer

The End of Manual Scanning

Automatic scanning receivers were an attractive feature of the new site in the 1970s. The marine radiotelegraph bands were broken up into smaller segments for calling coastal stations and for communications between the stations and ships. Before the advent of these electronic scanning receivers, however, operators had to hand-tune a receiver across the calling frequencies and listen for a call. This manual operation was performed on each radiotelegraph band, and normally one operator was assigned to a console designated for each band. All the bands are identified by their frequency in megahertz and are purposely selected for those harmonics which represent an even multiple of the lowest frequency possible in each of these bands. For many years, the early, unsophisticated equipment was audible on harmonics above the actual frequency in use, especially when broadcast near the receiving station. The assignment of the particular harmonics tended to prevent these stations from interfering with stations performing other services outside these bands. This explains the distinct call sign for each service performed on each frequency under the British Commonwealth Scheme.

The assignment of harmonic frequencies paved the way for the construction of shipboard transmitters which were tuned to frequencies with the help of precision crystals. For example, an alternating voltage can be created by using crystals when utilized in a feedback circuit where they oscillate at the mechanical frequency to which the material has been cut.[42] The resulting frequency can thus be utilized to feed a tuned electronic circuit. The tuning advantage of these transmitters derives from the fact that the crystal can be used to set the transmitter on many frequencies up through the different bands by using the harmonic or multiple of this crystal frequency. The band known as the two-megahertz band is found at the bottom end of the spectrum of these frequency bands, although VCS and most other stations did not monitor or communicate with ships on the radiotelegraph band assigned to these two-megahertz frequencies. The higher band frequencies are mostly even multiples of the two-megahertz band; hence, the two, four, six, eight, 12 and 16 megahertz marine bands. VSC could, on request, use the 22 megahertz band.

The automatic scanning receivers were solid-state or transistor equipment built in Dartmouth, Nova Scotia, and they worked superbly until the time these calling frequencies were terminated. Ships were later equipped with synthesized transmitters which were less restricting than

---

[42] Spurgeon Roscoe's manuscript *Radio Stations Common? Not this Kind.*

the old crystal equipment. Synthesized transmitters could transmit on any frequency in the marine bands. In the early 1970s, some foreign stations had already stopped the practice of scanning the calling frequencies and monitored only the one frequency on the "calling segment" of each band. All the operator had to do was sit back and listen to these units swing back and forth across the calling frequencies. When the call sign was heard, a switch on the scanning receiver halted the scanning process and remained locked on the frequency in order to obtain the calling ship's working frequency. Communication between the ship and the station was then possible when the coast-station operator released the scanning receiver to use the regular receiver, and the ship operator switched his transmitter to his working frequency. In the late 1970s and early 1980s, there were eight main operating positions for the operators at the VCS station.

During the 1970s, when the federal Department of Communications came into being, it took on the inspection, policing and examination duties previously conducted by the Ministry of Transport. Almost at the same time, licences became available to companies prepared to operate high-frequency, singleband communications direct from their offices to the vessels. Several of these companies installed the equipment, but the first to put it to use was the National Sea Products company. VCS was to receive occasional calls from these vessels when crew members wished to communicate directly with their homes, or perhaps when the captain was unable to conduct calls with the company radiotelephone. In fact, this technology resulted in no significant reduction in the radiotelephone traffic handled at VCS because many boats still sailed with only radiotelephone communications equipment.

Human Distress

As efficient and convenient as the telecommunications network was, the technology did not always work as intended. The fate of the *Angel B. Mills* is a case in point. The *Mills'* distress call never reached the ears of an operator at a marine radio station. And, while the crew survived, the loss of the vessel remains a significant event for the local population.

On August 10, 1956, after loading ice, fuel and stores at Sambro, Nova Scotia, for a swordfishing trip, Captain Harold Henneberry headed out. But three days later, he and his crew of six found themselves adrift in their dories. The *Angel B. Mills* had sprung a leak and sank. Their distress call was not heard because of interference produced by an approaching storm. While most fishing vessels had gone for shelter, the *Angel B. Mills* had taken water before being able to do so, effectively cutting off the battery supply that supplied the voltage for the lights and radio. For many days, the shipwrecked crew witnessed the raw indifference of nature, as they were lashed about in their little dories. They rowed and rowed above and below the peaks of waves, and it seems their courage never flagged, for on August 25, they finally reached the shores of Trepassey, Newfoundland. They had been in open boats for 10 days without food, and yet hunger had not unhinged their faith. The fate of the *Angel B. Mills* is one instance where humanity's inventions fell prey to an act of God, despite all attempts to reduce the risks.

A more recent incident involving Halifax Radio occurred in spring, 1976. The *Christmas Seal* was being used as a mobile X-ray unit sailing to Newfoundland outposts to assist in the prevention and cure of tuberculosis. The vessel was outbound from Halifax on May 13, 1976, when an explosion occurred in her engine room, and she burned rapidly and sank. The Halifax Traffic Centre received the distress call and relayed it to the VCS supervisor to notify all ships in the area. Meanwhile, the Coast Guard Regional Office dispatched several helicopters. VCS established communication with and notified the CCGS *Alert*, a search-and-rescue vessel with call sign CGDQ. A container ship named the *Atlantic Star* was also in the area, and changed its course to head to the scene. Although two crew members opted to head towards East Jeddore, Nova Scotia, aboard a whaler equipped with two outboard motors, all of the eight crew members were rescued without incident. The *Atlantic Star* picked up four men in a raft and two other crew members who had found refuge aboard a Boston whaler.

Equally unsettling is the story of the *Maurice Desgagnés*. On Wednesday, March 12, 1980, operator Bill Hall came to work at station VCS and secured the medium-frequency radiotelephone position for the first four hours of his shift—a routine shift. Hall, for some reason, was particularly thorough on that day, performing checks beyond the scope of his usual task list. He took a time check from radio station CHU in Ottawa and checked the setting of the clocks as he began his duties. Normally, this check is performed at 10:00 GMT, nearly two hours before Hall went on duty, and again at 18:00 GMT. Then, for no apparent reason, Hall turned the volume to full capacity on the 2,182-kilohertz receivers, the distress and calling frequency for the two megahertz radiotelephone band of frequencies. At about 8:30 GMT, a MAYDAY from the *Maurice Desgagnés* seared through the station.

Captain Gabriel Côté transmitted the call for help. The excitement in his voice was unusually discernible with the volume up as high as it was.

The *Maurice Desgagnés* was a small freighter, weighing 2,467 gross tons. She had just been purchased by what is now Groupe Desgagnés, a maritime transport company that was using the vessel for scheduled service between Eastern Canada and the West Indies. She had been in this service about a year when the call came in. The vessel, in accordance with regulations, carried a radio officer, but only while sailing in the West Indies. It seems that the operator had gotten off in New Orleans, Louisiana, and because of his absence, operators at VCS were unable to deliver messages to the ship.

The *Maurice Desgagnés* departed from New Orleans and was bound for Sept-Îles, Québec, with a large cargo of railway ties. As she approached southern Nova Scotia, she ran into heavy weather and high seas. There had been a number of storms plaguing the area in the previous few days—a typical March. On the morning of this March day, a huge sea struck the *Maurice Desgagnés* and caused some of her cargo to break loose in the hold. The loose cargo damaged some bulkheads and caused a crack in the deck. Water began to seep in.

Fortunately, the destroyer HMCS *Huron*, a newly built turbine-powered ship, was carrying out exercises only 66 kilometres away. The *Huron* acknowledged the distress call and immediately directed its course toward the cargo vessel. Racing to the scene, the *Huron* lost some lifeboats and incurred guardrail damage on the quarter-deck, a testament to the wrath and power of the Atlantic that day. Once the *Huron* was alongside the *Maurice*, Captain Côté felt the damaged ship could limp back into Halifax for repairs with the *Huron* giving escort.

After Bill Hall received the call from the *Maurice Desgagnés*, he shut down the remainder of the medium-frequency position and communicated only with those involved in the incident. At 11:45 GMT, when position rotation took place, Jim Best moved up from the 16 megahertz radiotelegraph position and took over from Hall.

The HMCS *Margaree*, an old destroyer escort, made its way to the scene to provide further assistance. At about 2:00 p.m., it became apparent that the *Maurice Desgagnés* would not remain afloat long enough to reach Halifax. A decision was made. The crew was taken off the ship by helicopter.

Spurgeon Roscoe, the next in line to guard the medium-frequency radiotelephone position at VCS, admits that "no one likes the radiotelephone positions. And if the static does not drive you insane, struggling to communicate in foreign languages will." After Roscoe got on, the HMCS *Huron* called in to confirm that the last of the 21-man crew had been safely evacuated. And just 20 minutes later, the *Maurice Desgagnés* sank beneath the waves.

Even with the best technology, seamanship remains the single most crucial factor in getting a ship from point A to point B. What, then, is the controlling factor for survival when nature steps in to claim a ship? Some say luck. Perhaps it was true in the case of the *Maurice Desgagnés*. The HMCS *Huron* was supposed to be sailing south on an exercise, but had developed some problems on the way and went back to Halifax for repairs. The *Huron* was testing the repairs with the assistance of the HMCS *Margaree* when the *Maurice Desgagnés* incident occurred. This fortuitous timing may well have saved the crew of the *Maurice Desgagnés*. The CCGS *Daring* was 33 kilometres away when the afflicted vessel sank; it would not have been able to reach the scene on time. It may have been able to rescue the crew from life rafts but, given that these same seas had killed the whole crew of the Japanese ship, *Raifuku Maru*, some years before, it is possible the seamen would not have survived in the rafts long enough to be picked up. The *Raifuku Maru* crew had tried to clear their lifeboats in similar weather conditions, but to no avail. It is unlikely that the crew of the *Maurice Desgagnés* could have done more.

Rum Running on the East Coast

Rum running in Canada got under way in earnest after the strong lobbying of American Senator Andrew Joseph Volstead saw the passing of the *Volstead Act* in the United States, prohibiting both the manufacture and sale of liquor. The U.S. Congress passed the law in 1919, and was strictly enforcing it by 1920. More than a decade later, writer D.G. Creighton said that the American government "had no experience in enforcing such legislation and no machinery to enforce it, and had not the slightest conceptions of the difficulties it would encounter..."[43]

Not surprisingly, Canada fell prey to the wave of legislative morality. All of the provinces except Québec had banned the consumption of alcohol by the end of World War I. The early 1920s saw massive evasion attempts through false medical prescriptions, boot-legging and home-brewing. Those who wanted to drink could easily do so, and rum running was supplying the demand. Extraordinary profits encouraged the development

---

[43] D.G. Creighton, "The Years of the Noble Experiment," *The Canadian Forum* (July 1931), p. 371.

of sophisticated black markets in both countries. Speakeasies popped up here and there, often owned by those who lobbied against the "vile repercussions of drinking."

Boats of all sizes were used both to carry the trade goods and to stop their delivery. Islands in the West Indies and St-Pierre and Miquelon, off the south coast of Newfoundland, proved ideal ports for loading the illicit goods. Some of the products manufactured here in Canada were exported on ships scheduled to return months later, ships that often made their way back within hours. Although at the time it was rumoured that Customs officials in Canada were cooperating in the racket, administrative records show little evidence of this. However, in important reports, names are left out and signatures are sometimes unintelligible scrawls.

With the Roaring 20s drawing to a close, the fist of poverty was preparing to fall in the Dirty 30s. With work practically non-existent in the 1930s, it stands to reason that any kind of income was welcomed, and some men worked the rum-running trade until hired on patrol vessels. Some wireless operators also got their start with the rum runners, later crossing over to the government side when legitimate jobs became available. Joseph Volstead could not possibly have predicted the degree of smuggling his efforts would spur in North America, and the Customs Service did not prevail in the crackdown on rum running.

On April 1, 1932, the marine section of the Royal Canadian Mounted Police (RCMP) came into active service and took over all the duties from the Customs' patrol vessels. The men who enlisted in the new organization wore a uniform not unlike the old uniforms worn by the Royal Canadian Navy. The marine section of the RCMP proved to be as fascinating as the "G" division which controlled the Yukon and the Northwest Territories. The "G" division was charged with the establishment of law and order, the "pacification of natives," the collection of customs and dues, and the suppression of liquor traffic. The famous RCMP supply vessel, the *St. Roch*, call sign VGSR, fell under the "G" division. Among its claims to fame, the *St. Roch* was the first vessel to circumnavigate North America.

Reading daily about the bread lines forming in the streets of North America, Cecil Kenny, an operator, knew well the hardships of the 1930s. He worked the lightships all he could in the summer, and he requested to stay an additional month on the *Halifax Lightship* to make the most money possible before season's end. Kenny then moved on to the RCMP patrol vessel *Fleur de Lis* to work as a radiotelegraph operator. It was on this ship that Kenny honed his skills for intercepting code. As deciphering was a time-consuming endeavour, Kenny requested the help of an assistant, George Guy, to handle the regular traffic. Even then, Kenny was unable to keep up with the ever-increasing workload and finally moved ashore to continue his deciphering. Little time elapsed before the smugglers were circled by RCMP vessels and trucks gathered at the designated landing sites, but a new code was always sure to surface shortly. "It generally took three or four months to break the code," says Kenny. "They'd have three or four alphabets. Even with a new code, you knew they were still saying the same thing. They were still talking about the same amount of kegs and the same landing spots." He listened to the clandestine stations and copied everything. One station usually operated more than others, handling in excess of 90 percent of the messages. The stations were principally located in Lunenburg, Sydney and Halifax, Nova Scotia.

The illegal stations used a letter and repetition system to transmit. Using the letters ABC for example: the A would be sent three times, followed by DE, the separation signal; then B three times, DE again, and finally C three times. The replying coast station would send the C three times, DE, and the B three times. All of this was decipherable, but the use of varied alphabets complicated matters for the authorities. The codes assured smugglers that they were indeed communicating with the correct stations and not with those operated by authorities.

Yarmouth, a port city on the southern tip of Nova Scotia, was a large rum-running port and the hub of a great portion of the illegal smuggling activities. In fact, some people earned a decent living installing wireless equipment on rum-running vessels. The stations were obviously unlicensed and they communicated with other illegal land stations. What's more, there existed an undeniable conflict of interest in the ranks when it came time to open an illegal station. For instance, a bank manager approached an officer in charge of the Saint John, New Brunswick, station, requesting that he send and receive messages for the rum trade. The officer is said to have declined, but passed the opportunity on to his operators. More out of need than opportunism, one accepted the offer and saw his attic converted into a radio room. Like several operators before him, he communicated with patrol vessels in the day and with rum runners at night. Kenny maintains that "we wanted the illegal stations to operate. It was the best way to know what the smugglers were up to. Our purpose was to stop the smuggling. With the large scale of the operation, it would have been pointless to arrest or fine someone running an unlicensed station."

The best rum-runner boats were small, fast and, in most cases, better equipped than the patrol vessels. Larger vessels were carrying the liquor cargo off the Canadian and American coasts, just outside international waters. From this point they discharged their cargo onto smaller vessels, often "Cape Island" types or so-called "Blacks" because of their black hulls. The preferred cargo boat was a converted schooner with the masts removed in favour of a motor. A converted schooner was ideal because it hove low in the distance, making it difficult for authorities to detect. The converted vessels were fitted with scaled-down direction finders the moment coastal direction finders came into service.

Authorities determined early which ships were rum running, and when RCMP crews sighted a smuggling vessel they would stay with the ship until an opportunity for an arrest arose. But as fog thickened around them, as it often did, the culprits were sometimes able to easily abscond. If there were sufficient grounds to seize a ship and arrest its crew, RCMP personnel gave chase. But, even with ships bearing names like the *Alachasse*, the RCMP cutters were slower than many rum runners, and the chase was often futile. "Stop in the name of the King!" did little to frighten the escaping smugglers. RCMP crews did fire their weapons at fleeing rum runners, but only on command.

At the time the RCMP's marine section was formed, improvements in aircraft design ushered in a "flying-boat service" between North America and Europe. Because of its lower fog densities, Shediac, New Brunswick, was chosen as a landing site for these aircraft. The flying boats carried radio operators who communicated with ground stations via radiotelegraph. A radio station at Shediac was constructed for air communications as well as for marine communications. The two services operated under different call signs, VFU for aircraft and VDS for sea vessels. The Shediac marine radio station also communicated message traffic it had collected from other stations to Halifax, VDH, on the three-megahertz frequency.[44]

Although the RCMP vessels normally communicated with Shediac and Halifax, they used other stations as well. The majority of their messages were in code, yet the RCMP vessels always used their international call signs—mandatory under international law. To obtain their position in low visibility, RCMP vessels requested that radio bearings be taken from their transmissions. An operator and direction finder were certainly welcomed assets on rum-runner boats. Even a good receiver would have been enough to outplay the RCMP, for coast stations provided a radio direction-finding service during this period. It was known as QTF, taken from the international list of Q signals. The

---

44 Spurgeon Roscoe's manuscript *Radio Stations Common? Not this Kind.*

International Q Code allows any ship or coast station to communicate regardless of language barriers. There are up to 70 three-letter Q codes, and abbreviations take the form of a request when a question mark follows. QTF means the "position of your station according to the bearings taken by the direction-finding stations I control is. . . latitude. . . longitude." All RCMP vessels fitted with wireless, including the *St. Roch*, had continuous wave equipment which had supplanted spark equipment. Most of the RCMP fleet was capable of transmitting on as high as the six-megahertz marine radiotelegraph frequency. The Marconi LTT4 was capable of going that high with slight modifications. The police fleet had 15 ships fitted with wireless, and the equipment standard at the time was again the Canadian Marconi units. The main transmitters were tuned to the usual wavelengths of 300, 600 and 800 metres. Even with this equipment:

> ...it soon became apparent that not only were the rum runners highly organized, they also relied heavily on radio to help off-shore fleets slip by cutters on patrol. There were about 50 unlicensed shore stations within 10 miles of New York City in 1930, (sic) maintaining a constant flow of illegal traffic. One of the best organized and most powerful radio networks did not belong to any government, but to the notorious Consolidated Exporters Corporation. The Corporation ran powerful shore stations in North and Central America. Its fleet alone exceeded that of the US Coast Guard.[45]

Soon radio communications, once the bane of efforts to enforce the law, became instead the weakness in the smugglers' chain of operations. Authority vessels were outfitted with HF receivers and improved direction finders. Cutters no longer patrolled thousands of hectares, conducting random searches; the patrol crews were using the same technology rum runners were using. And although the RCMP and United States Coast Guard operators began to win the "radio war" with the larger rum runners, the smaller rum-running vessels still squeaked through the web of security, bringing the liquor into Canada and the U.S.

Indeed, the RCMP marine section did well in hindering rum running. The fleet worked closely with the United States Coast Guard, but neither force could accurately claim responsibility for the illegal liquor trade's demise. In fact, it was none other than World War II that put an end to rum running. When Canada declared war in 1939, the

---

[45] Joseph V. Gardner, Ph.D., "Traditions and Transitions," Keynote address, March 31, 1995, at U.S. Coast Guard Communications station CAMSLANT/NMN, Chesapeake, VA. *The World Wireless Beacon* (Society of Wireless Pioneers, vol. 7, no. 2, June 1995), p. 4-6.

marine section, both ships and personnel, went to the Royal Canadian Navy and the Marine Division of the Royal Canadian Air Force. The rum-running vessels were also appropriated for the war effort. One such rum-running ship, the *REO II*, now located in the Fisheries Museum of the Atlantic at Lunenburg, Nova Scotia, was classified as an auxiliary minesweeper during the war.

The end of the war brought improved equipment and techniques, including radar. The post-war period saw increased reliance on aircraft radio communications needs, especially VHF and UHF. With the advent of communications satellites for automated wireless and of weather satellites, the roles of both the Coast Guard operator and Morse communications began changing radically. But as Joseph V. Gardner put it, "the mission will always stay."[46]

Yarmouth

Because of the prevalence of fog and strong tidal currents, mariners have always experienced great difficulties ascertaining their position when navigating the south-west coast of Nova Scotia, especially around Cape Sable and the Lurcher Shoals. In the early 1920s, the Department of Marine and Oceans decided to carry out tests in the Yarmouth area, hoping to establish a direction-finding station. A site was chosen at Rockville, near Yarmouth, and construction began in November, 1923. St. Paul Island also had a direction-finding station which had opened earlier, in September, 1923. The Rockville direction-finding station started giving bearings to vessels on January 5, 1924. The station was put to full use by vessels plying the Bay of Fundy and by fishing trawlers on the nearby banks. With the help of the Rockville direction-finding station, vessel masters in the Boston-Yarmouth service made their entrance into Yarmouth Harbour in the face of some severely adverse conditions. A landline telegraph connection ensured a link with the wireless office in the Halifax dockyard.

During wartime, the Department of Transport established submarine signal stations in Louisbourg and Yarmouth, Nova Scotia, and Negro Head, New Brunswick. Several developments came with the war. For instance, a chain of automatic radio-beacon stations was maintained to supplement the direction-finding service. The stations were located at all points where such aids were necessary to assist navigation. In a given area they were arranged, where possible, in groups of up to six, all transmitting at consecutive intervals on a common frequency. This allows navigators to

---

[46] Ibid., p. 6.

obtain six (where possible) bearings consecutively to establish their location. Around this time, there were 52 marine radio beacons in operation—26 on the east coast, 17 on the Great Lakes and nine on the west coast.[47] Several of the radio beacons were synchronized with fog alarms located at the same point for distance finding in foggy conditions.

Following the development of the direction finder for on-shore use, came the direction finder for on-board use. The traditional direction finder presented some problems in overcoming the effect of ships' funnels and cumbersome masts, and other large structures. Ship-borne direction finders worked in tandem with shore-based beacons. Radio beacons were, in effect, radio lighthouses with a range of some 125 kilometres. The first series of Canadian beacons was installed at Cape Bauld, Belle Isle Straits, Cape Ray, Cabot Straits, Seal Island and on ships located off Heath Point, Anticosti Island, Sambro and Lurcher Shoals. Initially the coast radio beacons consisted of spark-type equipment and they obtained their power from the supply of the fog alarm, operating during fog only. Later, four transmitting tubes were used for the beacon. Each was rated at 50 watts of output and was arranged to work in a back-to-back, self-rectifying circuit.

In 1961, the direction-finding services at Belle Isle, Cape Race, Camperdown, Canso, Saint John and Yarmouth were discontinued. Seven years later, the opening of Yarmouth marine radio became a reality. Most of the traffic at VAU was comprised of fishing vessels. Much like the Sydney centre, Yarmouth boasted radiotelephone on MF, VHF DF and NAVTEX starting in 1994. The station had five remotely controlled sites, two fewer than Sydney.

In June, 1997, Yarmouth Coast Guard Radio and Saint John (previously a traffic-management centre), combined to form the MCTS centre at Saint John, New Brunswick.

The International NAVTEX service is the coordinated broadcast and automatic reception on 518 kHz of maritime safety information by means of narrow-band direct-printing telegraphy using the English language.[48] Due to limited resources and Canada's huge size, the system in Canada had to be automated. This service does not require people, spelling yet another blow to the traditional role of the marine radio operator.

---

47 Department of Transport Annual Report, 1951/52, Telecommunications Division, p. 154.

48 International Maritime Organization, *Solas, Consolidated Edition 1992* (London: International Maritime Organization, Bath Press, 1992), p. 379.

Sydney and Charlottetown

A marine radio station opened at North Sydney in 1907. In its beginnings, Sydney Radio, VCO, was owned and operated by the Marconi Wireless Telegraph Company of Canada, under contract to the Department of Naval Service. It was perched on Harvey's Hill, exposed to every storm for which the Gulf is so noted. Besides communicating with ships at sea, the station worked with Sable Island and Cap-aux-Meules. Sydney linked Cape Ray and Pictou year-round, and linked Heath Point during the navigation season. In 1957, along with other Marconi stations, it was transferred to the Department of Transport. In 1965, it moved to the Sydney airport.

Once it was decided to divide marine radio and aeradio stations into separate entities again, the marine services at Sydney airport were transferred to a new facility at the Coast Guard College in 1988— approximately 25 kilometres from the airport. All telegraphy in the area is handled by the Sydney MCTS centre.

More stations were integrated in as MCTS streamlined its operations. The Charlottetown Coast Guard radio station closed on January 31, 1996, and its services were amalgamated at the Sydney MCTS centre. The original marine radio station was built at Cape Bear, Prince Edward Island, in 1905. Its purpose was to maintain contact with the government steamers, *Minto* and *Stanley*, while on winter service between Prince Edward Island and the mainland. Cape Bear, VCP, kept a close vigil over the Northumberland Strait. The Department of Marine and Fisheries saw considerable savings when the *Minto* and *Stanley* were first equipped with wireless, and the opening of Cape Bear led to more savings. The facility was to serve fishing fleets in the area as well. VCP closed in the early 1930s to reopen some years later.

In the mid-1950s, marine radio operations were combined with air services at the Charlottetown airport—call sign VCA. Another site was established by the Canadian Coast Guard at Bell's Hill, near Montague in autumn, 1984, a time when the Maritimes Region assumed control of Charlottetown Marine Radio, formerly under Transport Canada's Air Administration.

At the time, the station provided increased VHF radio communications capability as it operated remote sites at Cape Egmont, Point Escouminac, North Cape and the base station at Bell's Hill. A MF site at Harrington was also controlled from Charlottetown Radio.

Halifax Coast Guard Radio

Halifax Radio VCS became Canadian Coast Guard Radio Station Halifax on October 1, 1975. In 1980, the station averaged 12,000 contacts per month. Earlier, in June, 1979, operators on the coastal stations were tied to the Canadian Coast Guard. This smoothed the way for the separation of combined aeradio and marine radio stations into distinct entities once again. In May, 1988, Halifax Coast Guard Radio once again required larger accommodations because of an increase in traffic and workload. It was the largest and busiest Coast Guard Radio station in Canada at the time. Until recently, it was staffed with 36 operators, five communicators, 10 electronic technicians and clerical support staff. In the not-so-distant past, radio operators could communicate with ships as far away as the Indian Ocean and the Arctic using the Morse code. The last Morse message on 500 kHz, which was the last ever broadcast from the Halifax station, went out on November 19, 1996:

> Final broadcast on 500 kHz. Thank you for your patronage over the years. The Radio Operators of VCS wish you a safe voyage. 73 de VCS AR VA.

Raising the Marconi kite, Signal Hill, St. John's, Newfoundland. Marconi (far left) and his men as they prepared to receive the first transatlantic wireless transmission from Poldhu, England, Dec. 12, 1901. (National Archives of Canada, C5943)

A museum display of a typical five-kilowatt wireless coast station, the industry standard from 1904-20. (Courtesy of the Marconi International Marine Communications Co., Ltd.)

A museum display of a typical one-kilowatt wireless coast station, the industry standard for less powerful units from 1904-20. (Courtesy of the Marconi International Marine Communications Co., Ltd.)

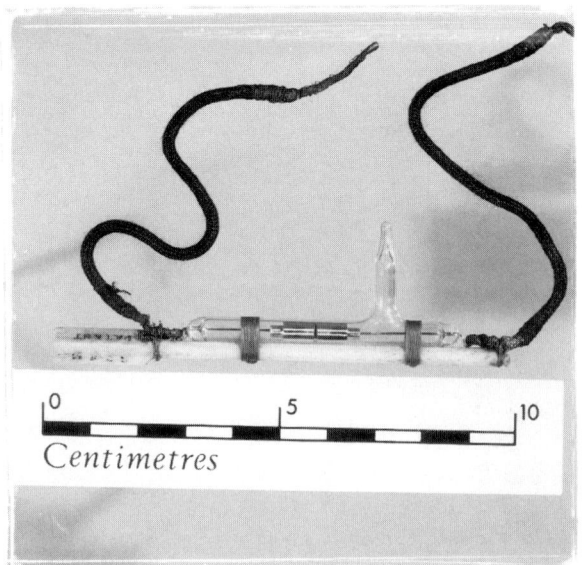

The coherer from the original receiver on the cableship *Mackay-Bennett*, assigned to study the useful range of the Camperdown station. Marconi installed the transmitter and receiver on the *Mackay-Bennett* in 1899 when the vessel was sent to New York to observe and report the famous yacht race between Sir Thomas Lipton's first *Shamrock* and the defending *Columbia*. (Courtesy of Dalhousie University Archives, Thomas Raddall Collection)

A log entry of Camperdown radio, call sign HX, later became VCS, recording the station's participation in the distress communications of the *Republic*, MKC, after she collided with the *Florida* on January 23, 1909. *Florida* was not fitted with wireless. The distress call CQD was inaugurated on this tragic day. (John Rae)

Pointe-au-Père, VCF, was key to the rescue of 465 passengers in the 1914 *Empress of Ireland* disaster, c. 1907. (National Archives of Canada, PA21377)

In June, 1913, the steam carrier *Caesar*, owned by Hellyer's Steam Fishing Company, Ltd., Hull, England, was the first fishing vessel to be fitted with wireless equipment. (Courtesy of the Marconi International Marine Communications Co., Ltd.)

Army personnel using heliograph signalling equipment at the Citadel in Halifax, Nova Scotia. The heliograph was one of the many communications systems used before the advent of wireless telegraphy, c. 1914. (National Archives of Canada, PA112391)

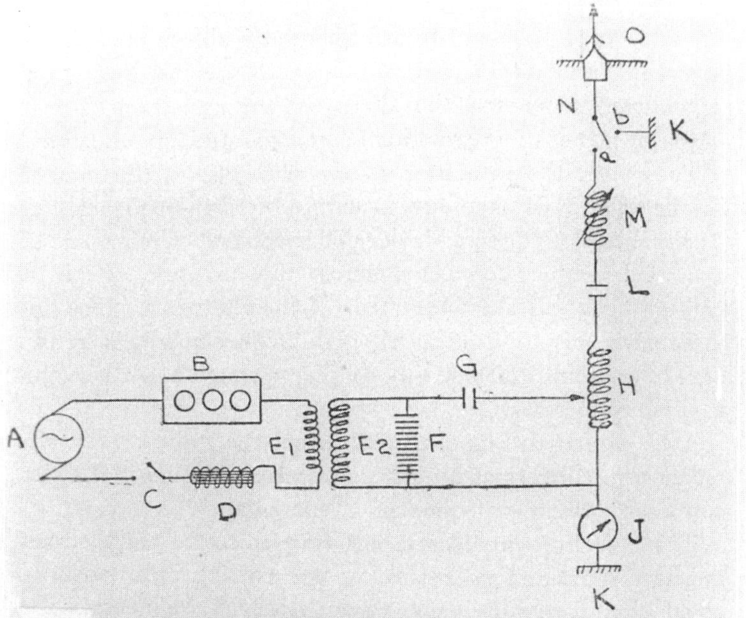

—DIAGRAMATIC REPRESENTATION OF A QUENCHED SPARK TRANSMITTER.

A 500 frequency alternator.
B Switchboard controlling alternator.
C Morse Key.
D Resonance choke coil.
$E_1 E_2$ High frequency transformer.
F Quenched spark gap.
G Excitation capacity.
H Excitation and coupling inductance.
J Aerial hot wire ammeter.
L Aerial shortening capacity.
M Aerial lengthening inductance.
N Protective lightning switch—
 Position a aerial to earth k.
 " b " apparatus.
O Aerial leading in insulator

From Brown's Signal Book, 1917. (John Rae)

The wireless room on the Italian vessel *Guisseppi Verde*, 1918. Radio officers stand beside the Marconi five-kilowatt Battleship Transmitter first manufactured in 1910. (Walter Hyndman)

A mock-up of the wireless room of the *Carpathia*, the lone rescuer of the *Titanic's* survivors, 1996. (Courtesy of the S.P.A.R.C. Museum)

A Marconi 10-inch spark transmitter, Marconi Wireless Telegraph, London. Widely used from 1904-20, this type of equipment was phased out following the arrival of tube equipment. (Courtesy of the S.P.A.R.C. Museum)

Leyden jars, type of capicitor used with the spark transmitter, 1996. (Courtesy of the S.P.A.R.C. Museum)

The Marconi magnetic detector was used to receive signals from other stations. It worked alongside the spark transmitter, 1996. (Courtesy of the S.P.A.R.C. Museum)

Marconi MSTI receiver with an array of Morse keys, 1996. (Courtesy of the S.P.A.R.C. Museum)

Marconi auto alarm detectors became popular after the 1906 Berlin conference made them mandatory on smaller ships. Automatic alarms triggered the sounding of three bells, signalling a ship in distress in the area. But the system was perhaps too efficient —because of excellent propagation conditions, the ship apparatus could be activated by distress calls originating thousands of kilometres away, 1996. (Courtesy of the S.P.A.R.C. Museum)

Wireless operator Thomas H. Raddall relaxing at Camperdown radio, Nova Scotia, 1922. Like many of his colleagues, Raddall became frustrated with the Canadian Marconi Company and quit shortly after this photograph was taken. He later became a celebrated author whose works were set in remote marine radio station sites. (G.E. Champion)

In the early days, operators and their wives landed at Pachena Point, a west-coast station, in this manner. Woman unknown, 1913. (Courtesy of the S.P.A.R.C. Museum)

The west-coast station Pachena Point as it stood in 1910. The radio building is on the right and the dwelling for operators is on the left. (Courtesy of the S.P.A.R.C. Museum)

Some pioneers of the west-coast wireless service. Jack Bowerman, later Superintendent of the service, sits second from the right, back row. Contrary to the wireless networks along the east coast and the Great Lakes System, the Pacific network was established by the Canadian government rather than the Marconi Company, c. 1913.
(Courtesy of the S.P.A.R.C. Museum)

Operator Walter Howard at the Gonzales Hill station, Victoria, British Columbia, 1911.
(Courtesy of the S.P.A.R.C. Museum)

Off the northern tip of Vancouver Island, Triangle Island is wide open to Pacific gales. Masts made of felled trees brought over from the mainland held the aerials, c. 1912. (Courtesy of the S.P.A.R.C. Museum)

On October 22, 1912, Triangle Island experienced a severe windstorm with 160-kilometre-per-hour gales which broke the anemometer as well as the shaft holding the four rotating cups. Operators could only wait out the storm. Later that year, the Department of Marine and Fisheries wedged heavy 8" x 8" shores against the sides of the buildings. Steel cables were secured over the roofs and workers made fast to cement deadmen in the ground. (Courtesy of the S.P.A.R.C. Museum)

Operating position at Triangle Island, VAG, c. 1913. (Courtesy of the S.P.A.R.C. Museum)

The west-coast Cape Lazo station, VAC, in 1913, a site still occupied by today's Comox MCTS centre. (Courtesy of the S.P.A.R.C. Museum)

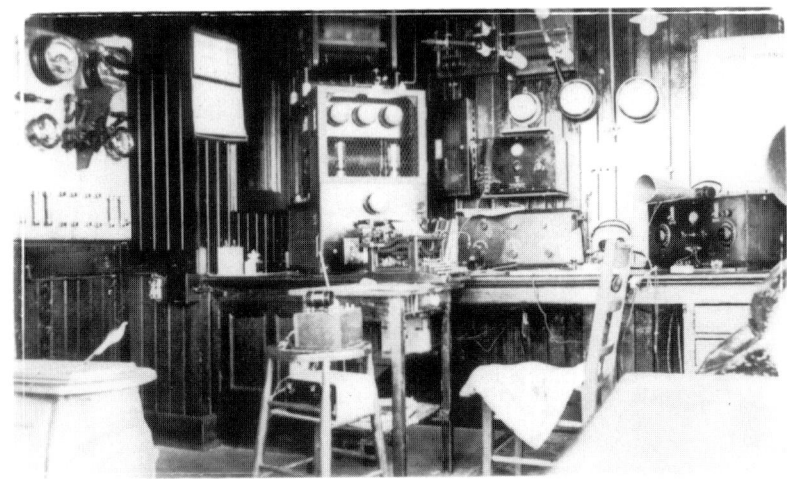
Cape Lazo's operating position, 1925. (Courtesy of the S.P.A.R.C. Museum)

Radio operator Jim Harker and his wife at Alert Bay, 1915. During the war years all government radio stations fell under the Naval Service. Civilian operators were required to wear naval uniforms. (Courtesy of the S.P.A.R.C. Museum)

Alert Bay, VAF, in the very beginning. Operator Jack Bowerman (left) standing next to an unidentified operator, 1913. (Richard Loeb)

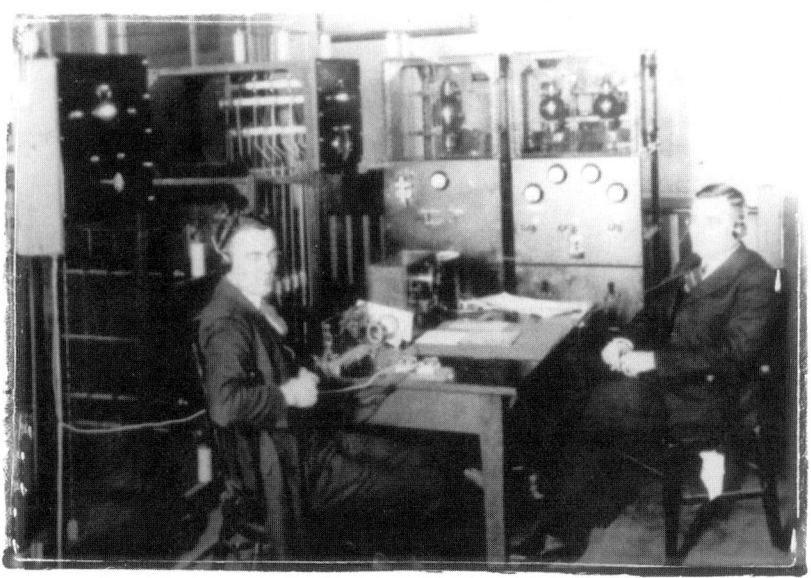

Radio operators, Len Crowe and Jim Harker, working the Vancouver station, VAB, 1923. (Courtesy of the S.P.A.R.C. Museum)

Radio operator Jim Harker operating what was then the new radiotelephone installation of Vancouver radio, VAB, in 1925. The receiver was the famous Northern Electric Peanut tube set. (Courtesy of the S.P.A.R.C. Museum)

An early teletypewriter which transmitted and received written messages and data via radio relay systems. Originally developed by Frederick G. Creed, a British inventor, in the late 1890s. More often called a teletype, this instrument was used to great effect in Canada's marine radio network. (MCTS collection)

Engine room, Estevan Point station, VAE, 1916. This is a single-diesel engine which was started by compressed air. Electric starters had not yet been invented, and in some cases operators, depending on the type of engine, had to rotate the flywheel until the starter was set to spark. They primed the engine with raw gas, checked that the oil lubricator drip cups were full, and adjusted the drip rate. Finally, they switched on the ignition by closing a small knife switch, turned on the fuel line and spun the flywheel. Even after all this, operators were never sure that the engine would start. They activated the engine to supply energy to the transmitter or to charge the batteries. (Courtesy of the S.P.A.R.C. Museum)

Canada's first wireless operators had no other means of improving the quality of their transmitting other than to emulate those blessed with a natural ability for the art. Jim Myrick was a model for many on Canada's east coast. Myrick is seated on the left transmitting, while Cyprien Ferland is seated on the right receiving at the opening of the transoceanic beam service from Drummondville, Québec, to overseas, October, 1926. The other men are unknown. (Cyprien Ferland)

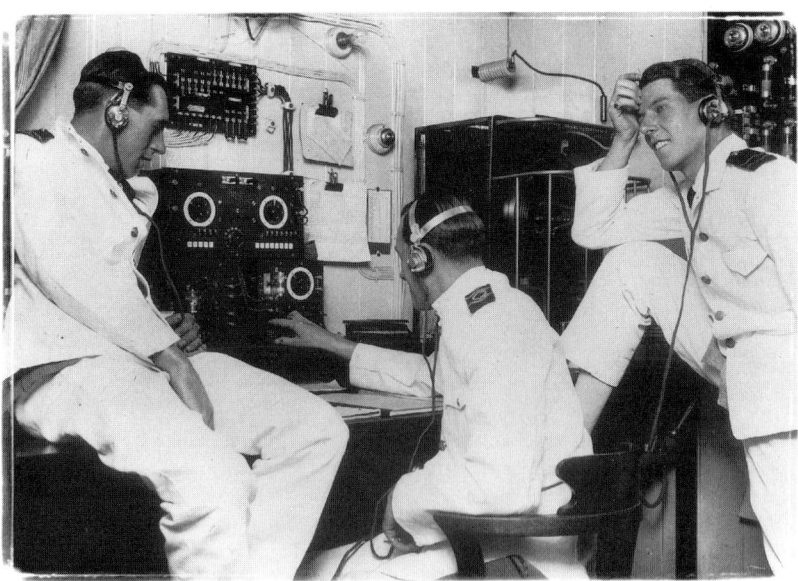

Unidentified wireless operators on the Canadian Pacific's *Empress of France*, 1923. (Canadian Pacific 10354)

Wireless room of the Canadian Pacific's *Empress of France*, 1923. (Canadian Pacific 10452)

Radio operator Warren Hagar operating Chebucto, VAV, 1926. (Warren E. Hagar)

Radio operator Alexander McLean operating Belle Isle Radio, VCM, winter, 1925. (Reay Bridger)

Ottawa wireless station, VAA, used for first transatlantic service. Halifax VBQ maintained a continuous radiotelegraph service between Halifax and the Ottawa radio station, c. 1920. (National Archives of Canada, PA92358)

In 1920, the first broadcast station, XWA (later CFCF Montréal) went on air. Marconi owned and operated the station whose call letters are still used today by one of Montréal's English-language television broadcasters, c. 1920. (National Archives of Canada, PA44182)

In the late 1920s, as the North gained acceptance as the fastest route into or out of Canada, radio stations sprang up in strategic locations, and Archibald N. Fraser, Chief Engineer of what was called the Radio Branch, headed the implementation of the North's web of radio stations. Fraser, man in leather coat in the middle, is surrounded by his team of technicians en route from the east coast to the North. (Archibald Fraser)

The Northwest Territories' Nottingham Island, VCB, station under construction, 1927. (National Archives of Canada, PA55537)

Radio direction-finding station at Cape Hope's Advance, VAY, in 1928. (National Archives of Canada, PA44106)

Marconi low-frequency transmitter, Churchill marine radio station, VAP, c. 1930. (Archibald Fraser)

Royal Corps of Signals station at Aklavik, Northwest Territories, 1925. (National Archives of Canada, PA100551)

In the distance, the *S.S. Larch* and the *Stanley* berthing off the coast of Nottingham Island in July, 1927. The Department of Marine and Fisheries sought Marconi's expertise in 1904, when three government ships were outfitted with wireless stations: the *Stanley*, the *Canada* and the *Minto*. (National Archives of Canada, PA55540)

Radio communications played a key role in capturing murderer Albert Johnson at Aklavik. (Johnson, the blond man in the centre, is shown here at the Ross River trading post some time before his crimes.) Known as the mad trapper of Rat River, Johnson killed an RCMP officer and wounded radio personnel and other officers before being captured. It was not until Wop May, a famous Canadian aviator, got involved that the mad trapper was arrested, c. 1928. (National Archives of Canada, C39883)

A Sikorsky VS-44 "flying boat," much like the *Untin Bowler*. In the late 1920s, expeditions having to do with the Canadian North gave point-to-point circuit telegraphy its place in the sun. (Bill Stempel, Greenwhich, Connecticut)

Shediac Aeradio, 1932. Because of its lower fog densities, Shediac, New Brunswick, was chosen as a landing site for the flying boat service. Flying boats carried radio operators who communicated with ground stations via radiotelegraph. The Shediac radio station was constructed for air communications and, later, a section for marine communications was added. The two services operated under different call signs, VFU for aircraft and VDS for sea vessels. (Warren Hagar)

The lake carrier *Gleneagles* at Fort William, June, 1930. (George Adamson)

Wireless cabin of the "Laker" *SS Valley Camp*, 1935. (George Adamson)

Wireless cabin aboard the *SS Harmonic*, VGRQ, 1938. (George Adamson)

Another view of *Harmonic's* wireless cabin, 1938. (George Adamson)

Unidentified wireless operator at Port Burwell, Ontario, c. 1938. (George Adamson)

Operating position at Camperdown Radio, VCS, c. 1938. (C.R. Spracklin)

Camperdown staff repairing antennae after an ice storm, 1938. (W.H. Wooding)

Bill Baker operating Camperdown Radio, 1938. (W.H. Wooding)

British Freedom before its participation in Convoy BX-141, c. 1940. (World Ship Photo Library)

The *Martin Van Buren*, participant in the Boston/Halifax convoy, after it was hit by acoustic torpedoes from the German U-1232 submarine, under Captain Dobratz, which simply lay in wait for ships entering or leaving Halifax, 1945. (Rex Garrison)

Unidentified women opening cases of contraband from the wreck of the *Martin Van Buren*. Nova Scotia, 1945. (Evelyn McCready)

The Estevan Point station, VAE, on its perch on the west coast of Vancouver Island. During World War II, the lighthouse and nearby buildings were fired on by a Japanese submarine, the first attack on Canadian soil since the War of 1812. Material damage was incurred, but no lives were lost, c. 1950. (Courtesy of the S.P.A.R.C. Museum)

Point Grey, the predecessor to the Vancouver MCTS centre, opened in 1908. Decades later, Point Grey gained some prominence when, during the Second World War, female operators were hired to work at the station. A shortage of operators had become a serious problem and extra people were needed as the government worked to intercept the Japanese (or KANA) code, c. 1937. (Courtesy of the S.P.A.R.C. Museum)

Operations room
Halifax Radio, CFH,
1947. (Bob Palmer)

Receiver site of Halifax
Radio, Albro Lake,
Nova Scotia, 1947.
(Bob Palmer)

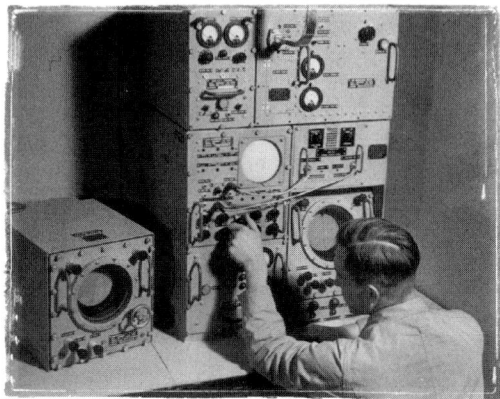

The operator's console of the type 268 radar designed and built by the National Research Council. The type 268 radar afforded a mere 6.6-kilometre coverage, 1944. (Courtesy of the National Film Board)

Type 268 radar antenna at Camperdown, VCS, September, 1949. (Courtesy of the National Research Council)

Early one foggy morning in 1952, the *Italia*, with 1,500 passengers, narrowly escaped tragedy in Halifax Harbour thanks to the low-range type 268 radar. (World Ship Society)

Radio operator Dave Clarkson at radar plotting position, Camperdown Radio, 1956. (Alex Murray)

Radio operator Stan Cairns operating the teletype, replacing the old landline Morse system with CN/CP and Western Union, 1956. (Alex Murray)

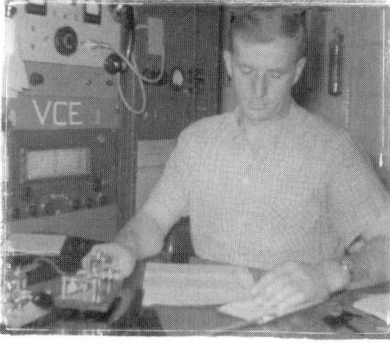

Operator Samuel Johnson operating Cape Race, summer, 1959. Cape Race was in contact with the *Titanic* as she sank off Newfoundland's Grand Banks. In 1965, after 61 years of continuous operation, the station became obsolete. In the early days of magnetic and crystal detector receivers, most westbound vessels plying the Atlantic came within range of Cape Race and its call letters VCE. (Courtesy of Samuel Johnson)

Outside view of Marconi station at Belle Isle. The longer building housed the radio station. The four short masts supported the direction-finding loops. The longer mast in the centre supported the main antenna, 1956. (Samuel Johnson)

Fame Point, VCG, 1950s. In spring, 1904, Marconi employees built the station and installed a standard one-kilowatt Marconi spark-gap transmitter, a Marconi 10-inch induction coil serving as emergency transmitter, and a Marconi magnetic receiver. *Saturday June 25, 1904, 8:25 p.m., first communication with* Parisian *bound east, 23 miles west. 9:33 p.m. Finish with P. read 16, sent 1. Communication perfect.* This is the first entry of the original Fame Point log and the first ship-to-shore communication on the continent. (Courtesy of Lloyd Nelson)

Officer in charge Lloyd Nelson, spring, 1956. Nelson became the last Morse operator at Fame Point before the power lines went down due to ice damage. Fame Point was already slated to move to Rivière-au-Renard in the Department of Transport's bid to centralize all wireless services. (Courtesy of Lloyd Nelson)

Radio operator Philip Lacasse taking a ship report by radiotelephone at Fame Point, 1955. (Courtesy of Lloyd Nelson)

Radio operator Claude Gervais on duty at Fame Point, 1956. (Courtesy of Lloyd Nelson)

The radio station at Resolution Island, Northwest Territories, with its inverted "V" antennae. The highest tower on the right is the low-frequency antenna and the shortest is the high-frequency antenna, 1960. (Raymond Douville)

The 290-metre transmission tower at Resolution Island, c. 1960. (Émile Bonneau)

Frobisher Bay's domestic circuit, September, 1961. (Raymond Douville)

Radio operator Raymond Douville operating the marine circuit at Frobisher Bay, 1961. (Raymond Douville)

Radio operator Dave Green operating the point-to-point circuit at Frobisher Bay, 1961. (Raymond Douville)

Dave Green, Raymond Douville and unidentified radio operator in the operations room of the Frobisher Bay marine and aeradio station, 1961. (Raymond Douville)

Frobisher Bay, 1961. (Raymond Douville)

Blue Nose II radio room with radio officers Henry Whitehead (standing) and David Wail. The RCA 5U station was manufactured in the 1950s and installed on the *RCMP Wood*, the *Bounty* and the *D'Iberville*. The RCA unit had a 150-watt output, c. 1965. (David Wail)

Mike Doutaz (foreground) and Reg Cavanah operating the radio room aboard the Canadian Coast Guard vessel *Vancouver*, 1968. (source unknown)

Radio officer Spurgeon Roscoe operating the radio room aboard the *Gypsum Prince*, 1970. (Captain Claude Marcel)

Operations room, Halifax marine radio, VCS, Camperdown, just before closing and moving to Ketch Harbour, Nova Scotia, 1970. (Teed)

Killiniq Coast Guard radio station, c. 1975. (source unknown)

George MacAlpine who, some operators claim, still haunts the site of the Killiniq station, c. 1975. (Martin Grégoire)

The loss of the *Aigle D'Océan* in August, 1975. Twenty minutes after the *Aigle's* distress call, the engines of the Canadian Coast Guard icebreaker *Norman MacLeod Rogers* were ready. The *Rogers* had left Frobisher Bay (Iqaluit) bound for Ungava Bay on August 19,1975, to conduct a scientific mission. The ice-reconnaissance helicopter went ahead to assess the *Aigle's* situation. Fewer than 10 kilometres separated the two ships, 1975. (Hubert Desgagnés)

The crew of the icebreaker acted quickly to bring the five survivors on board. But in their search for the less fortunate, they found only the bodies of Richard and André Paré—two other men remained missing and are presumed drowned. Adding to the disaster, the icebreaker's reconnaissance helicopter never returned, 1975. (Hubert Desgagnés)

The *Rogers* crew found the skeleton of the helicopter on the rocks at Killiniq. It had crashed and both the pilot and mechanic were dead. The undisturbed wreckage reposing on the rocks of Killiniq serves as a reminder to this day. In all, the death toll that fateful day totalled six, 1975. (Hubert Desgagnés)

M/V *Christmas Seal* in serious distress off Halifax, Nova Scotia, 1976. The M/V *Christmas Seal* was used as a mobile X-ray unit sailing to Newfoundland outposts to help prevent and cure tuberculosis. The vessel was outbound from Halifax on May 13, 1976, when an engine-room explosion caused her to burn rapidly and sink. The Halifax Traffic Centre received the distress call and relayed it to the VCS supervisor to notify all ships in the area, 1976. (Wamboldt-Waterfield)

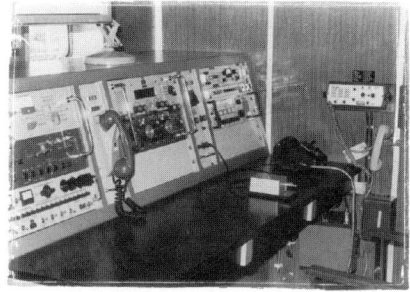 

CGS *Cape Rogers'* radio room, VCBT, 1977, one of the last to require a radio officer. (Canadian Shipping and Marine Engineering)

The operations room at VCS, 1977.

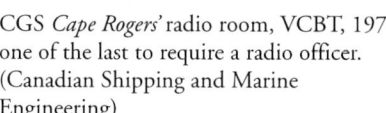

Florence Gulak operating the MF position. Gulak was the first woman to operate station VCS, 1977. (John Rae and Paul Britton)

COME QUICK DANGER — A HISTORY OF MARINE RADIO IN CANADA

Transmitter building at Halifax Coast Guard Radio VCS, Pennant, 1980. (John Rae and Paul Britton)

The crew of the M/V *Maurice Desgagnés* being lifted by a Department of National Defence helicopter. The M/V *Maurice Desgagnés* departed from New Orleans and was bound for Sept-Îles, Québec, with a large cargo of railway ties. On March 12, 1980, as she approached southern Nova Scotia, the M/V *Maurice Desgagnés* hit heavy weather and high seas. Several storms had plagued the area in the last few days, 1980. (C.F.B. Shearwater)

The M/V *Maurice Desgagnés* just before it sank. On the morning of March 12, 1980, a huge sea struck the M/V *Maurice Desgagnés* and caused some of her cargo to break loose in the hold. The loose cargo damaged some bulkheads and caused a crack in the deck. Water began to seep in, 1980. (C.F.B. Shearwater)

Vessel Traffic Management Station, "Halifax Traffic," and the Chebucto Head Lighthouse, 1980. (John Rae and Paul Britton)

Inside view of "Halifax Traffic," 1980. (John Rae and Paul Britton)

 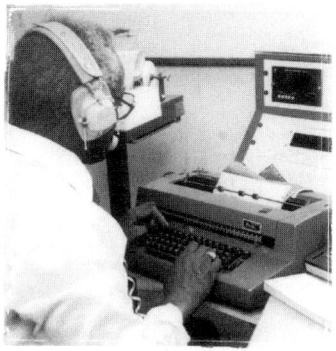

Pierre Boisvert (left) and Claude Deschenes at the Québec City Vessel Traffic Management Centre, c. 1980. (source unknown)

Radio operator Percival Bourne operating Montréal marine radio, VFF, from Dorval Airport, c. 1980. (Courtesy of Percival Bourne)

Operations room of Halifax Coast Guard Radio, 1985. (source unknown)

Staff of Coast Guard station and community of Rivière-au-Renard celebrating the anniversary of VCG's 90 years of service. VCG was the call sign of Fame Point marine radio, the first station to go on the air in North America, 1994. (Charles Dufresne)

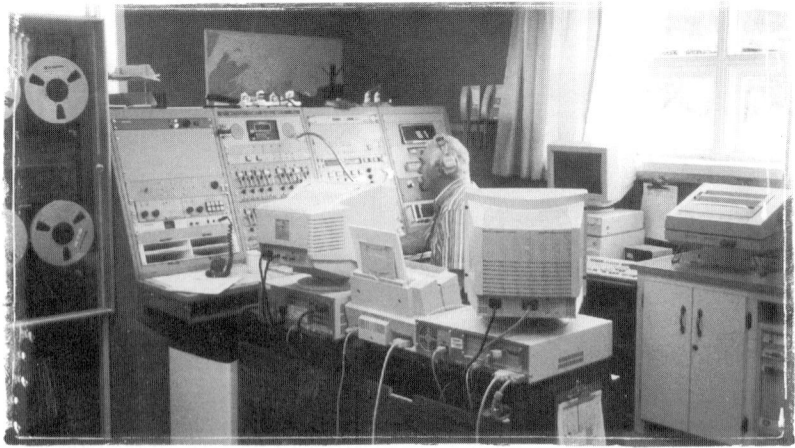

Radio operator Terry Simms at console of St. Anthony Coast Guard radio station, Goose Cove Road, which closed in July, 1996. (source unknown)

Cap-aux-Meules MCTS's transmitting and receiving antennae. Small house, top left, is the ex-Marconi wireless station, 1997. (Gisèle Bettez)

Thunder Bay MCTS officer, Lori Bedford, at console on the official opening day of the new centre at the Coast Guard base, 1997. (Lea Barker)

Chapter 4
Radio and the Great Lakes System

Author Alvin Toffler wrote, "we have a destiny to create." He could have easily been referring to the pioneering drive behind the development of marine radio. Throughout history explorers have reached beyond and brought forth new possibilities from which to fashion our destinies. When it came time for a new means of communication, Guglielmo Marconi devised it. In doing so, Marconi brought increased safety to mariners. His company, in concert with others, established radio stations around the world, not the least of which were the Marconi stations of the Great Lakes.

Economics have for centuries motivated decision making, and profit making has long had its hand in shaping history. After the Second World War, a great economic boom fueled by foreign investment necessitated a reliable transportation network into the heartland of Canada and the U.S. The idea had been touted for many years, but had met with opposition from Canadian and American port cities, as well as from railway companies. Halifax, for instance, stood to lose its reign as the gateway to Canada. From the earliest periods of colonization, the Maritimes port cities together were a great economic force because of their strategic locations. Louisbourg, Nova Scotia, for instance, was a stronghold in the era of New France. Then the post-Second World War economic boom saw the development of the St. Lawrence Seaway and the Great Lakes System into a continuously navigable route, promoting and increasing international trade. Ships from 60 countries began to ply the very waters that British and American warships had travelled not so long ago. As traffic increased, vessel traffic services were implemented in the Great Lakes region and marine communications continually improved.

The St. Lawrence River/Great Lakes System, extending eastward from Anticosti Island, Québec, to Thunder Bay, Ontario, at the west end of Lake Superior, grew into a commercial giant. In 1982, the average value of the total cargo moving on the system at any one time totalled $10 billion. Larger lake carriers moved freight equivalent to that of a loaded four-kilometre train. The maximum vessel size allowed in the Seaway was 730' x 75'. These dimensions accommodated 85 percent of the ships in the world when the Seaway opened in April, 1959. Today, only 8 percent of the world's fleet is small enough to transit in the Seaway and Welland Canal locks. What's more, market conditions are also responsible for the system's decline. The fall of the Soviet Union and subsequently its currency system, for instance, has drastically reduced grain movements out of Canada.

Other Canadian waterways, however, are experiencing an upturn in market conditions. The North, for example, had been on a slow development path while the Hudson's Bay Company had a stronghold on the vast area. As the North slowly became accepted as the quickest route into or out of Canada, it became home to several radio stations in strategic locations. Archibald N. Fraser, Chief Engineer of what was called the Radio Branch in the 1920s, headed the implementation of a web of radio stations in the North. Suspicions of rich resources in these northern lands were well founded. The Canadian North is rich in resources, and mine exploitation continues to this day to contribute to the area's development. Northern ports continue to profit greatly from the inception of trade routes for the exploitation of raw products. And Fraser would surely agree that coastal radio stations have long played important roles, ensuring the safe movement of these products. Radio stations-cum-MCTS centres still provide vessels transiting Canadian waters with weather broadcasts and information on ice conditions and obstructions to navigation, and maintain a distress-frequency watch.

The old expression "coast station" is a term borrowed from Marconi's design. According to Marconi, stations that were to work ships at sea had to be close to the coast. It appears that Marconi did not realize that ground conductivity is an important factor in determining a radio station's communication range. At the time, it was believed that the close proximity to the coast reduced the coastal refraction of received signals; this would easily lend itself to direction finding. Time and better equipment later debunked this theory. As discussed earlier, Coast Guard stations once operated from airports, far removed from the coast.

In the early 1900s, the government started opening stations along what is now the Great Lakes System's coasts. The first station to open was Port Arthur, Ontario, in November, 1910, and the Marconi Wireless Telegraph Company of Canada managed and operated the installation.

The government paid for the construction, with the agreement that it could take over the full operations from Marconi whenever it wanted. The Port Arthur station proved immediately useful when the Steamer *Dunedin* of the Inland Lines ran ashore on Isle Royale on December 7, 1910. In direct response to this incident, a scheme was drawn up to set up a chain of stations each approximately 300 kilometres apart, from Port Arthur to Kingston, Ontario. The Kingston station, as originally planned, had sufficient range to communicate with Montréal, linking the proposed system with the east-coast system and allowing straight-through communication to Cape Race, Newfoundland. The Canadian Great Lakes marine radio stations were constructed at:
- Gore Bay (Manitoulin Island)
- Kingston VBH
- Midland VBC
- Point Edward VBE
- Port Arthur VBA
- Port Burwell VBF
- Port Colborne
- Port Stanley
- Sarnia (replacing Point Edward) VBE
- Sault Ste. Marie VBB
- Thunder Bay (replacing Port Arthur) VBA
- Tobermory VBD
- Toronto VBG

Thunder Bay

In 1962, the Port Arthur, Ontario, station—now Thunder Bay—was combined with the aeradio station at Fort William. The aeradio/marine radio station came under the authority of the Department of Transport's Air Services Branch in Winnipeg. The names of the two towns—Port Arthur and Fort William—became insignificant when, in 1975, they amalgamated to form Thunder Bay. The combined Department of Transport station continued its operations at the Thunder Bay airport until April 1, 1986, when it was relocated to the Thunder Bay Post Office Building and commissioned as a Canadian Coast Guard Radio station. Thunder Bay was the last station to retain combined status (that is aeradio and marine radio working shoulder to shoulder). On April 1, 1997, the station started to operate in the Coast Guard base, located in the western outskirts of the city. The services of both Wiarton and Sault Ste. Marie were integrated with the new site shortly after it moved into the base.

Port Burwell

Sitting at the mouth of Otter Creek and 66 kilometres west of the Long Point Lighthouse, Port Burwell was long considered one of the best harbours on the north shore of Lake Erie. It was the Canadian Pacific Railway branch terminus and, for many years, large coal stocks were piled on the West Pier by Imperial Fuels and the Valley Camp Company.

The original wireless station at Port Burwell was about half a kilometre east of the main harbour light. The operations building contained both the main and emergency spark transmitters, and the magnetic detector receivers which were later replaced by crystal receivers. An electric generator, driven by a hand-started gasoline engine, charged the batteries and supplied power to the transmitter. In the 1920s, vacuum tube receivers came into use, followed 10 years later by hydro-electric power, and then ICW[49] tube transmitters. In no time, communications were scheduled with radio operators posted at both Long Point Lighthouse in the north-eastern part of Lake Erie and the Southeast Shoal Lighthouse down in the western part of Lake Erie.

Like operators at other stations, Port Burwell operators had to be well versed in both the International and American codes. Port Burwell had a tie-in with the Canadian Pacific telegraph lines for many years preceding the teletype. After the teletype, came radiotelephone. Ship-to-shore radiotelephone meant that CW operators were no longer needed on ships. The situation was further improved by the development of duplex calling systems which allowed vessel masters to communicate with any land-based telephone subscriber. In the early days, spark communications for the Great Lakes were all on 410, 425 and 187 kHz. As for radiotelephone channels, they were first established on the medium- and high-frequency bands from two to six megahertz, which were replaced by the VHF and UHF channels. Operating the medium- and high-frequency channels was difficult because of the constantly changing atmospheric conditions.

Port Burwell and Tobermory were the last stations to be served by hydro-electric power. For some time, before the conversion was complete, ship operators remained more likely to give their messages to other hydro-powered stations rather than wait for the shore operator to make his way to the engine room to start his gas engine in order to supply power to the transmitter.

---

[49] Interrupted Continuous Wave.

In the early part of this century, serious soil erosion along the Lake Erie shore in the vicinity of the Port Burwell station progressed to such an extent as to imperil the safety of the station. In February, 1921, it was finally decided to move the buildings and masts to a new location about 213 metres further inland and a 1.2-hectare site was expropriated on which to build them. Only one mast was re-erected at the new site; it used an umbrella type of aerial. The station was put back in service on May 4, 1921.[50] A double residence was provided for two staff members and their families by the Midland, Ontario, contractor who built the stations at Kingston, Midland and Port Burwell. Although the Royal Navy was closely associated with the operations of the Great Lakes System during World War I (for most of the war, the militia guarded the stations), the normal staff at the station in peacetime consisted of four wireless operators. Work included the transmission of weather forecasts, transmitted twice daily at 10:30 a.m. and 10:30 p.m. Notices to Shipping were also transmitted on the high-power spark transmitters. When, in 1957, Marine Radio Aids and Aviation Radio Aids Services were amalgamated under one management at the Department of Transport, the Port Burwell facility was integrated at the airport just north of Port Burwell. The call sign VBF was no longer used.

Point Edward and Sarnia

The Point Edward station, with the long-held call sign VBE, opened in 1913. Point Edward marine radio stood approximately 200 metres from the beach and, not unlike Port Burwell, was also a victim of bad design. Built on the edge of an escarpment, the station towered perilously over Lake Erie waters. Over the years, the flow of lake water into the St. Clair River was such that it gradually eroded the shoreline, and by 1950 it was clear that the station might be washed into the river. Noise levels from nearby Sarnia also caused signal interference problems.

By the 1950s, the erosion and interference had become too serious to ignore. What's more, the equipment at VBE had become obsolete. VBE moved to Camlachie in 1954 as a marine radio station. In 1982, it moved again, this time to the federal building in downtown Sarnia. Then, on January 24, 1996, it was integrated in the new MCTS centre, located in the same building.

Long before Sarnia's beginnings though, the Department of Naval Service was forced in 1917 to make some early changes to the Point

---

[50] Department of Marine and Fisheries Annual Report, 1922.

Edward station. Because of actions taken by the Hydro-electric Commission of Ontario, the frequency of the Point Edward station's power supply was changed from 60 to 25 cycles. Consequently, new transformers and motors had to be installed to supply power to the radiotelegraph transmitting apparatus.

Radiotelephone

In 1945, duplex radiotelephone facilities began operating at Sault Ste. Marie to serve the ships plying the Sault canals. Radiotelephone-equipped ships could carry on two-way telephone conversations with any telephone on shore. Similar installations were already operating at Port Arthur and Toronto. The increasing use of this popular technology meant that the available frequencies were soon overloaded with interference. To circumvent this problem, government technicians carried out tests to determine if the use of ultra-high frequencies, employing frequency modulation (FM), would eliminate much of the interference. We know today the clarity and precision of FM signals, but when FM was first introduced, and while AM was enjoying wide-scale use, stations used a very broad band of 120 kHz. Over time, bands were narrowed down, just wide enough to carry communications with little interference. The narrower the band, the more efficient the use of the radio spectrum, and the more power directed to the meaningful part of the signal. By 1940, 76 lake carriers were equipped with radiotelephone technology on the Great Lakes.

Radiotelephone came to the Pacific coast first—as early as 1924. It was implemented specifically for communication with the tug boats and other craft working the lumber trade. Ship-to-shore radiotelephone service was provided from departmental stations at Vancouver, Merry Island, Cape Lazo, Alert Bay and Prince Rupert. By 1930, 49 tugs were equipped with radiotelephone. A decade later, 165 tugs and many other small craft were equipped with radiotelephone.[51]

On the east coast, a Radiotelephone Aids to Navigation Broadcast service to fishermen was inaugurated in April, 1928. By 1940, the majority of fishing vessels were equipped with radio receivers to take advantage of the service.[52] Several stations were used for this purpose: Louisbourg, VAS, Sambro Lightship, VGX, Saint John, New Brunswick,

---

51 VHF/FM radiotelephone was installed on 28 Canadian Coast Guard vessels. By 1962, all Canadian Coast Guard vessels had VHF communications. New high-frequency AM radiotelephones were installed on eight of these 28 vessels and 23 launches associated with the larger ships.

52 Department of Marine and Fisheries Annual Report, 1940.

CHSJ, Yarmouth, Nova Scotia, CJLS. For its part, Louisbourg, using a 14,000-watt radiotelephone transmitter, broadcast on 434.4 metres at 3 a.m. and at 12:00 noon, E.S.T. Messages included weather information, storm warnings and a synopsis of market tendencies concerning fish prices. The power of this station allowed fishermen well out into the Atlantic, to the east of the Grand Banks, to receive all the information. The station at Saint John broadcast on 336.9 metres at 7 a.m. and at 11 a.m. During the summer months, the service was supplemented with the CGS *Arras*, CGFD, a boat which accompanied the fishing fleet and broadcast storm warnings and weather forecasts by radiotelephone. The Department of Transport added more stations such as the Halifax Lightship, VCX, which broadcast information on 322.4 metres at 7 a.m. and 12:30 p.m., with a range of 240 kilometres.

In the 1950s, commercial shipping on the Great Lakes and St. Lawrence River reached an all-time high. The increasing traffic resulted in unforeseen congestion in rivers and canals at either end of the lakes and on to Montréal harbour. Ship masters, shipping companies and both the American and Canadian governments were seeking ways to circumvent the problem. For its part, the Department of Transport delegated its power to the Canals Branch, which eventually laid the foundations for marine traffic control systems. The vessel traffic control systems were equipped with radiotelephone systems installed at the Guard Gate, above the Welland Canal locks, and in the district office in Cornwall.

Prior to the mid-1940s, most ships on the Great Lakes communicated by means of radiotelegraphy. With tube equipment, though, the radiotelephone technique really came into its own. Ship masters worked in tandem with the vessel control systems if they had good radiotelephone equipment on the bridge. Before radiotelephone technology, captains had to fill out a message form which was brought to the radio room and transmitted to a nearby ship—an involved process which precluded quick decision making in congested waters. It had long been evident that ships required good radiotelephone equipment directly on the bridge for the immediate use of the captain or responsible navigating officer.

Captains called each other to ensure that the way ahead was clear or to pace themselves in order to obtain eventual passage. Alternatively, captains found out where to anchor until the course was clear or the lock became available. There was no vessel control except at two Canadian canals; elsewhere captains compensated by cooperative effort. But with the increasing number of ocean-going ships entering the Great Lakes, cooperative effort soon proved insufficient to placate the fears of seasoned Lake goers. Most of the new traffic was under the command of foreign-registered masters, who had little experience sailing in these congested waters. The problem was compounded by the fact that most deep-sea ships did not have the correct radio equipment to communicate with the already established structure. Both American and Canadian masters felt the admission of salt-water vessels reduced safety, even when qualified Canadian pilots were at the helm.

In 1952, American and Canadian representatives met in Ottawa to take joint action. The Canadian group was headed by G.C.W. Browne, Controller of Radio for the Department of Transport, flanked by the department's marine radio engineers, Marine Services, Radio Inspections and representatives of the Dominion Marine Association. The American group was headed by Commodore E.M. Webster, Commissioner of the Federal Communications Commission (FCC). Webster was supported by the State Department, FCC radio engineers, United States Coast Guard and the Lake Carriers Association.

The delegates forged an Agreement for the Promotion of Safety on the Great Lakes by Means of Radio. From that point on, all ships, regardless of country or registry, had to be fitted with radiotelephone equipment capable of communicating at least 80 kilometres. The agreement made mandatory the installation of radio on the bridge, where the radio was set to maritime mobile low/medium frequencies—to wit, worldwide calling, safety, inter-ship and ship-to-shore channels. These improved communications standards added a new dimension to work on the bridge. For the first time, all ships received timely weather information and notices to mariners directly on the bridge. Canada, the controlling agent of the entrance to the upper St. Lawrence River and Great Lakes, was responsible for inspecting ocean-going ships to ensure they met the requirements of the Great Lakes treaty.

Also in compliance with the treaty, the department's coast stations across Canada were upgraded to meet with current industry standards. Remote transmitters and receiving antennae and corresponding remote receiving stations were installed. Duplexing facilities were also built, and telephone connections were tied into local telephone companies, affording crew members the possibility of communicating with any telephone subscriber in North America. What's more, ship owners were able to talk with their captains, no matter where the captains were in Canadian waters. Coast stations began to play a bigger, more helpful role than ever before.

As a direct result of the Great Lakes treaty, CW or Morse code was no longer used on the Great Lakes. It was brought back in the early 1980s, however, as the problem of several languages over the radiotelephone had become serious. Normal communications, with a Polish ship, for instance, could take up to two hours even with the use of the phonetic alphabet. Morse code was implemented at the Toronto station, the regional office at the time. But because of fierce AM interference coming from homes in the metropolitan region, Morse operations were transferred to Sault Ste. Marie. Since Sault Ste. Marie's services were integrated at the Thunder Bay MCTS centre, all Morse communications have since been handled from the new site.

By the early 1950s, the advantages of FM communications on the VHF band were gaining considerable international recognition. C.P. Edwards, then Deputy Minister at the Department of Transport, asked to try out VHF FM radio when he was vacationing at Georgian Bay. On board a friend's boat he was able to communicate with Midland, the first station to be fitted with FM; the year was 1952. The equipment at both the station and on board the craft was single-channel equipment operating on the international distress, safety and calling frequency of 156.8 MHz. Edwards was pleased with the results and thus began a transition period in marine radio communications in Canada. Shortly after, similar equipment was put in place at Montréal and Saint John (N.B.).

By the time the Seaway opened, many world ports were equipped to provide a wide range of services using the maritime mobile VHF FM channels, which had been designated by member administrations of the International Telecommunication Union. Ships of all registries had upscale FM communications. So, too, did Great Lakes carriers. VHF, and certainly FM, did much to circumvent the problematic effect of peak sunspot cycles on MF/HF propagation. MF communications from ship and land stations on the Mississippi and the east coast often interfered with communications on the Lakes.

Simplex push-to-talk radiotelephone service gave way to dual-frequency duplex service, which is similar to ordinary telephone service. Calls from any land-based telephone subscriber could be received on board ships. Skippers had only to give the coast-station operator the name and number of the person they wished to call. The new service also provided some interesting stories. For example, there was the yacht owner who called Kingston, VBH, to place a bet by proxy in New York. The man had laid down a large sum. The horse won the race, and immediately the owner held a large party on the boat to celebrate. The money, however, never arrived. Much to the anger of the boat owner, the message detailing the wager had fallen down behind equipment at the coast station. It was never sent!

The use of microwave radio relay stations by Canadian telephone companies assured the provision of many more telephone circuits at much reduced cost. This, along with the increasing popularity of VHF FM, enabled a complete restructuring of the marine radio service in the late 1950s and early 1960s. Other coastal stations began offering radiotelephone around this time as well—namely, Montréal, Québec City, Pointe-au-Père, Fame Point, Cap-aux-Meules, North Sydney, Canso, Yarmouth, Saint John and, later, Belle Isle and Cape Race— extending radiotelephone communications from the Great Lakes to the Atlantic.[53]

In the early 1960s, a new technique for high-frequency marine communications appeared on the scene. The new method was called single side band modulation (SSB). Because it increased the intelligibility of voice communications to and from ships at long range on high frequencies, the Department of Transport was quick to adopt the feature in its coastal and ship radio stations. For the first time, it became possible to make voice contact with a ship crossing the Atlantic at almost any point of her voyage. Propagation conditions still obscured the signal, but the capability of consistent ship-to-shore contact by voice greatly improved. The new technique increased user efficiency of the radio spectrum and significantly decreased the power needed for transmitters compared with the voice transmission techniques of the 1930s.[54]

Toronto and Cardinal

The original Toronto station, which opened in January, 1914, was located at the south-west corner of Toronto Island, more specifically at Gibraltar Point. When the need for duplex radiotelephone service became evident, a remote station for radiotelephone reception was built about a kilometre north of the coast station, in the direction of the Island Airport on Hanlan's Point. But soon the radio noise level created by appliances in homes on the island and by the industries and power lines along the

---

53 Department of Transport Annual Report, 1945.

54 R.C. Reardon, *Maritime Mobile Radio Communications and Navigation: From Marconi to Satellites*, Telecommunications & Electronics (Ottawa: Department of Transport, 1986), p.11.

shore severely limited the working range of the coast-station radiotelephone. The marine radio beacon transmitter beside the coast interfered with the long-wave operation of the coast station.

Later, the station was slated to move a few kilometres to Trafalgar, where radio noise level would be minimal. In 1952, the Toronto marine radio station at Trafalgar was completed and put in operation to provide a greatly improved service. From the onset, the new station had four times the range of the original location during day-time operations. At the Long Point radio beacon, a new power house was built and the station was completely renovated. The Gibraltar Point radio beacon was switched to remote radio control from Trafalgar, about 30 kilometres away.

The Cardinal coast station opened in 1960. It first began operating out of the two-car garage annexed to the unfinished station. The road on which the station was built, previously called County Line, was renamed Coast Station Road some time after Cardinal officially opened. The original GE transmitter was installed on Blair Road, two and a half kilometres out of town.

In spring, 1978, at a time when AM was being eliminated on the Great Lakes, the station at Kingston, VBH, was closed and "remoted" to Cardinal. Like many other Great Lakes stations, Kingston had been a Marconi station opened in the early part of the century.

Today's Prescott Coast Guard MCTS centre is an offshoot of the Toronto and Cardinal stations; in other words, Prescott came to be with the closing of both Toronto and Cardinal Coast Guard radio stations. Prescott first went on air in April, 1995—the official opening came later that summer, on July 7. The Coast Guard ceased its operations at the Cardinal radio station on March 29. The Toronto station closed several days later. Much of the equipment now housed in the Prescott MCTS centre was taken from both Toronto and Cardinal, with a few additions including a new computerized charting system.

Prescott's area of responsibility runs from east of Cornwall to the eastern end of Lake Erie, including the Rideau waterway, the Trent/Severn System and parts of the Ottawa River. Transmission sites are set up in Cornwall, Cardinal, Kingston, Cobourg, Trafalgar, Fonthill and Orillia.

VHF (Very High Frequency)

In 1968, the addition of a "remoted" transmitting and receiving facility at Bonaventure improved ship-to-shore communications in the vicinity of Bay des Chaleurs to Miramichi Bay, New Brunswick. The facility was controlled from Rivière-au-Renard. More communications improvements came soon after—this time, from the western end of Lake Ontario to the eastern end of Lake Erie, and on the Welland Canal when the Department of Transport "remoted" VHF facilities at Fonthill, Ontario. Each of these was controlled from Toronto. In the Hudson Bay area, the department launched a message and telephone service on VHF at Churchill, Manitoba. British Columbia's Strait of Juan de Fuca area also saw changes when the Victoria marine radio station relocated to Sooke, British Columbia, with the addition of a MF/VHF marine telephone service and a VHF message and broadcast service.

In 1982, the effectiveness of Coast Guard Radio Stations was greatly improved, chiefly because of the VHF peripheral communication facilities commissioned at:
- Point Riche, Newfoundland (controlled from St. Anthony)
- Bonavista, Newfoundland (controlled from St. John's)
- Cape North, Nova Scotia (controlled from Sydney)
- Natashquan, Québec (controlled from Rivière-au-Renard)
- Pointe-au-Baril and Killarney, Ontario (controlled from Wiarton)
- Mt. Helmcken, British Columbia (controlled from Victoria).

The facilities provided a range of 40 nautical miles (74 km) along Canada's coastlines.[55]

VHF radiotelephone service was later extended because of the declining use of Morse code. Five remote sites were constructed and ready to go live in 1983. The implementation of VHF continued on the British Columbia coast. Perched on mountain tops, nine VHF radio transceiver sites were constructed to offer a reliable public-correspondence service along Canadian coastal waters off British Columbia, reaching up to 40 nautical miles (74 km) offshore. The three-year project cost $6.8 million.

The plan to provide complete very high frequency ship-to-shore coverage of Canadian waters on the Great Lakes and Georgian Bay was completed in 1974. Also, to improve safety, both the United States and Canada agreed to cooperate in radiotelephone communication on the Great Lakes. The Department of Transport also implemented a program to provide mariners with continuous access to weather and dangers-to-navigation information, through means of continuous transcribed broadcasts on VHF. The information is still broadcast by today's MCTS centres across Canada. As well, radioteletype came to be the main alternative to radiotelegraphy for the handling of high-seas message

---

55 Department of Transport Annual Report, 1982.

traffic. Later, Transport Canada's Telecom and Electronics directorate gave Canada a marine ship-to-shore radioteletype service at Halifax and Vancouver.[56]

The "Ghost"

A radio operator who receives a distress call may have to stay with the mariner for many hours. Getting a Search and Rescue (SAR) response team to specified coordinates is no small matter in the usually adverse conditions. What operators experience in such crises has been coined the "ghost." They are the only link to possible victims—not in body but in spirit.

Dealing at once with panic-stricken mariners on one frequency, and response teams, doctors, hospitals on another, operators must maintain composure—this is key to a successful rescue. As time elapses, operators know too well the increasing gravity of such situations. Sometimes, the rescue operation is futile because of forbidding sea conditions. Usually, though, the rescue is successful. With distressed voices and even screams at the other end of the line, operators can do little but stay with the victims and provide that link, the "ghost." Without minimizing the work of SAR personnel who risk their lives every day, operators have to deal with the situation from another standpoint. Not at the scene to witness for themselves, they must imagine the situation and sometimes imagining is far worse than the reality.

George Olmstead was stationed at Sault Ste. Marie in summer, 1977. It was early evening when the words, "Help me! Help me!" came in from a shipboard radio. Waves up to two metres were lapping over the small sailboat heaving on Lake Huron, North Channel. A woman's cries seared into Olmstead's earphones. Her husband was overboard. The grief-stricken woman froze and so too did her finger on the press-to-talk switch. She could not hear Olmstead. Time was elapsing. "Help me help you," Olmstead thought to himself. He was her only link to safety. He stayed with her; an hour had now elapsed. He finally obtained landmarks from her in order to send Search and Rescue personnel. Given her panicked state, coordinates were definitely out of the question. She was brought to safety; her husband, however, is presumed lost at sea.

While the workload of radio operators diminished with the advent of new technology, by the same token, the effectiveness of Search and Rescue coordinators increased. For instance, the COSPAS-SARSAT,

---

[56] Department of Transport Annual Report, 1974.

a satellite-based system for detecting and locating emergency distress beacons, as well as other computer programs, including one with the ability to find the telephone numbers of neighbours of lost persons, all reduce response time.

"Critical incident stress" is a term used to describe the effects of traumatic events. Many Canadian Coast Guard employees are at risk simply by virtue of their occupation. A Transport Canada publication entitled *Critical Incident Stress Management* has rated radio operating as one of the occupations most prone to critical incident stress.

Programs to help those in such high-stress jobs have been implemented slowly. In the Pacific Region, a stress-management program got the go-head in 1994. The sheer volume of traffic on the Pacific coast coupled with the geography of the waterways raises the risk of incidents which, in turn, causes work-related stress to increase.

"The Pacific, from Singapore and Malaysia to the west, to Japan, Hong Kong, and Korea to the north, Hawaii and California towards the east and Australia to the south has become the fastest growing community on the planet, representing one third of the world's population."[57] Strangely, the authors of *The Story of English*, from which this passage is taken, left out British Columbia. Indeed, British Columbia is Canada's fastest growing area. The shipping world regularly steers for its ports. And Vancouver MCTS officers are no strangers to the workload of 10 vessel movements per hour while a Canso officer, in Nova Scotia, for instance, may deal with just one vessel movement during the whole day. Work-related stress of this scope could have MCTS officers handing in their resignation simply for fear of making a mistake. It has happened.

---

57 Robert MacNeil, et al., *The Story of English* (London: Faber and Faber, 1992), p.368.

Chapter 5

The Sinking of the Aigle D'Océan and the Arctic Region

The Canadian Arctic has long had the distinction of being one of the world's "weather factories." But every summer the ice in this frigid region melts a little, allowing ships to pass through the otherwise impenetrable waters. Vessels laden with grain and minerals take advantage of the time to make their exit to Europe, but servicing the numerous bases and Inuit villages is a major occupation for ships plying the Arctic waters. Coasters, most of them from Québec, performed that function through most of the 1970s.

The summer of 1975 was like any other, except for the absence of ice in the Hudson Strait region, making it a slow summer for icebreakers. The *Norman McLeod Rogers*, a Canadian Coast Guard icebreaker based in Québec, was on duty in the sober Arctic region that summer. Its 12,000-horsepower engine was put to little use as few ships required an escort. The *Rogers*, as it is most often referred to, left Frobisher Bay (Iqaluit) bound for Ungava Bay on August 19, 1975, to conduct a scientific mission.

On that same day, all hands were busy aboard the *Aigle D'Océan*, a coaster from St. Joseph-de-la-Rive. The crew had finished unloading in Quaqtaq, a village on the northwest tip of the Ungava Peninsula. Quaqtaq was the last stop of the final voyage for the vintage coaster, built in 1919. Once home it was to head straight for the scrap-yard. The nine crew members working on the tug-cum-cargo vessel were quite content, and well they should have been, for the voyage was coming to a close. At 8 p.m. the barges were stowed in the hold and Captain Francoeur manoeuvred the vessel to leave its berth.

"Gale warning," came over the *Aigle*'s shipboard radio. Captain Émile Lavoie of the *Norman McLeod Rogers* repeated the message: "Gale warning, north-eastern winds." This weather forecast from Resolute

Radio repeated a previously received warning of an approaching storm with predicted winds of up to 50 knots. Captain Francoeur decided to head for Killiniq, a small island in the vicinity, and to wait there for better sailing conditions. Soon the winds raged at 25 to 30 knots, the temperature dipped down to the freezing point. The date was August 20. Aboard the *Aigle D'Océan*, the men felt the ship move violently as they plied out of the Strait. All that night and the following morning the north winds forced the small ship of 43 metres to chart a path through peril. Captain Francoeur was worried: "it won't be pretty when we get to the Labrador coast with a swell on the side. We can wait at Port Burwell till it calms down."[58]

At noon, Julien Tremblay was up for duty in the engine room of the *Aigle D'Océan*. The diesel motors were running smoothly, but the rocking of the waves grew steadily worse. Tools slid about easily with the tossing of the ship. "We'll clean up at Port Burwell; it'll be more quiet," thought Tremblay.

At 1:25 p.m. Hubert Desgagnés, third officer on the *Rogers*, went up to the wheel-house to get some news on the *Aigle D'Océan*. Desgagnés was especially concerned this day because his cousin Julien Tremblay, with whom he had studied at Sydney, Nova Scotia, for two years, was aboard the *Aigle D'Océan*.

"*Norman McLeod Rogers*, this is *Aigle D'Océan*. We are sinking! Come help us! Fast."

The *Aigle D'Océan*, while changing course for Killiniq, had tipped to one side. But instead of rolling normally, the ship listed abruptly and did not come back to port. The third officer, Pierre-Paul Bouchard, checked the hold for unlatched barges. All was in its place, but his gaze locked on the metre-high water washing through the hold.

Captain Francoeur well understood the gravity of the situation. The crew prepared to abandon ship, whose list by this point was at 25 degrees. They hailed the *Rogers* immediately. Land was but five kilometres away. Captain Francoeur knew that the ship would never make it. "We can't wait anymore. The starboard lifeboat must be launched right away."

Rain blinded the now desperate men as they fought to save their lives. As soon as the lifeboat dropped into the sea it began to roll at the mercy of the confused waters. The men were unable to hold onto the

---

58 The *Aigle D'Océan* account appears courtesy of Hubert Desgagnés. Port Burwell, a village on the island of Killiniq, was named after an operator who worked there. Unfortunately, research has not yielded his full name. A station was opened there in the 1920s, before relocating to Resolution Island.

restraining lines and, as one crew-member was forced to let go, the craft suddenly nosed into the water. When it resettled in a horizontal position, the lifeboat was filled with water. The coaster was listing severely, rendering it impossible to use the portside lifeboat. Assuming that it would float, because of its watertight casing, seven of the nine-man crew jumped in, but the small craft capsized after catching under the ship's rubbing strake. The men fell into the sea.

Back on the *Rogers* all hands worked feverishly. Twenty minutes after the first call, the engines were ready. The anchor was raised and the ice-reconnaissance helicopter went ahead to assess the situation plaguing the crew of the coaster. Less than 10 kilometres separated the two ships.

Fifteen minutes after the lifeboat capsized, the crew of the *Aigle D'Océan* noticed that the cook, Marcel Tremblay was missing. Gilles Baril decided to swim up to the ladder, but the strong currents swept him away—he never made it. The others witnessed as they were making their way back on the sinking boat.

By now the rail of the main deck was disappearing under water, allowing the men to set foot on the inclined deck. At times the list reached a full 40 degrees, making the hike to the portside bulwark harsh. Four men, very cold by now, rejoined the captain and his officer Jeannot Belley, both holding onto the bow on the outside of the railing. Alone, Richard Paré was clutched on the inside bulwark, too exhausted to move. His brother, André, was still submerged in frigid 2° C waters.

Homing in on the scene, the stem of the icebreaker laboured through every wave. Then, radio contact was lost. Had the *Aigle D'Océan* sunk?

"Radar contact 35 degrees to starboard." Gerard Belley, the first officer of the *Rogers*, saw an echo on the radar display. Minutes later, through the drizzle, the scene of the *Aigle D'Océan*, listing badly, came into view—the crew of the *Rogers* looked on. Visible were the men clinging to the side. The radar antenna was still turning and the lights were still on.

Captain Lavoie of the *Rogers* brought the ship windward of the *Aigle D'Océan*, all the while maintaining a cautious distance of approximately 75 metres. Manoeuvring was complicated because the current raged opposite the wind, which blew confused waves hither and yon. With every roll, the ship leaned more. Pierre-Paul Bouchard forced the men to keep moving to avoid going into shock. But hypothermia was settling in regardless and it was beginning to take its toll.

The wind blew the canvass over the hatch covers extremely taut; so much so, it seemed it would tear at the seams. A last cloud of black smoke rose from the stack; the radar stopped; the ship was going down.

Then came a sound like a gunshot. The heaving line of the *Rogers* was fired, uniting the ships. The *Rogers* sent an inflatable raft to the seven crew members, or rather, six crew members—without a sound, Richard Paré had fallen into the sea once again.

Julien Tremblay jumped first as the raft was moored to the railing. Pierre Hamel fell in the water and Julien Tremblay, sparing no effort, grabbed him. André Paré was not so lucky. He had been submerged in the frigid waters for some time. And, like his brother, he was exhausted and the cold Ungava Bay waters had numbed his limbs. The two brothers died of exposure.

With the ship rolling further toward capsizing, it was with his two feet on the keel that the captain leaped into the raft. He was the last to jump, unwittingly observing the age-old tradition. For a few moments, the survivors became panicked when they realized that the raft was still moored to the quickly sinking coaster. In the excitement, nobody could find a knife to cut the nylon rope, and it was with his dentures that the captain managed to cut the tether.

Very quickly the stern sank in a geyser of water. *L'Aigle D'Océan* lay on its side once again, as though reconsidering its decision to die, but the weight of the water had the last word. The bow rose to the sky and in a gush of white water the ship disappeared, leaving only a raft and assorted debris on the surface. In total, just 30 minutes had passed since the arrival of the *Norman McLeod Rogers*.

The crew of the icebreaker acted quickly to bring the five survivors on board. They searched for the missing crew members but found only the bodies of Richard and André Paré—two other crew members remained missing and are presumed drowned. And as though the disaster was determined to dominate, the helicopter did not return. The *Rogers* crew eventually located the aircraft, but it was only the skeleton of the helicopter that they found on the rocks at Killiniq. The chopper had crashed and both the pilot and mechanic were dead. In all, six men lost their lives that August day. The undisturbed wreckage of the helicopter reposing on the rocks of Killiniq serves as a reminder to this day.

Although horrific, the incident could have been worse. The network of radio stations in the North has for decades afforded the safe movement of ship traffic. Not only do the stations provide distress watches and weather broadcasts, such as the one that finally reached the *Aigle D'Océan*, they also transmit vital information about ice conditions and movements. Ice observations and weather reports would be useless if not instantly distributed by way of telecommunications. The northern seas are frozen and impassable by normal vessels for much of the year. There are of course other constraints that limit navigation, such as the severe wind storms which may occur during spring and fall, exacerbating difficulties in ice operations. In addition, some areas are marred by vexing fog triggered by warm water currents. For example, Nottingham Island and Resolution Island at the west and east ends of the Hudson Strait may have fog for up to 18 days a month between June and September. Such conditions make ocean transport hazardous without shore-based assistance.

Nottingham Island

The first meteorological and ice observations conducted for the purpose of assisting shipping were performed on July 1, 1927. The Nottingham Island radio station, call sign VCB, made the first broadcast. The station was staffed by two operators and a cook, all relieved once a year with the arrival of the icebreaker. In addition to personnel, the icebreaker brought a year's worth of supplies.

The station was located on the southern end of the island which in all is approximately 53 kilometres long by 20 kilometres at its widest part. The island lies at the western end of the Hudson Strait at the entrance to Hudson Bay and the Foxe Channel. Nottingham Radio opened in 1927 to provide communications to ship expeditions in the summer months.

In its later years, the station operated 24 hours a day from early July to late October, with three operators on staff. The rest of the year only two operators remained to operate a point-to-point circuit with Frobisher Bay (now Iqaluit). Like other stations, it relayed both synoptic weather observations and domestic and departmental traffic. From 1969 until its closure in 1970, the station operated only as a weather observation post with a staff of two operators. The only outside communication available was when aircraft could land, weather permitting, using either floats in the summer or skis in the winter.

Because of the vastness of the North, there were great distances between coast stations. These greater distances, coupled with the propagation difficulties encountered, made radiotelegraphy the most reliable means of ship-to-shore communication; and at the time, the slowly changing communications pattern made it likely that radiotelegraphy would continue. Radiotelephone, on the other hand, was used to good advantage over shorter distances, and was especially valuable in the coordination and direction of outpost re-supply operations. In the late 1960s, ship radio stations, such as those of the Canadian Coast Guard with transmitters rated at 100-watt output, could expect to obtain a coverage range of about 415 kilometres. Smaller ships such as coasters, operated with reduced coverage. Atmospheric noise and fading during the hours between sunset and sunrise also reduced coverage. In the late 1960s, VHF was not widely used as a supplement to the two and four megahertz radiotelephone communications. However, it was reliable for communication between Canadian Coast Guard icebreakers and vessels under escort and was used very effectively at the beachheads during outpost servicing operations.[59]

Working in tandem with the radio stations, icebreakers have long been opening up routes through the otherwise impassable ice, but other Canadian Coast Guard vessels such as the *C.D. Howe*, for example, provided medical and dental care to isolated bases and Inuit villages. In the busy days of Nottingham Island, its limited population of nine, three of whom were government employees, did not warrant a live-in doctor much less a dentist. The arrival of the *C.D. Howe* surely placated some ailments. Medical consultation was also available from Frobisher Bay Hospital. However, the island dwellers had neither schooling nor shopping, although they could order goods by catalogue or message to Frobisher before each scheduled flight. Shipments of such goods came via sealift in the summer, while smaller shipments arrived with each incoming aircraft in the winter.

It is telling that, in 1969, the operators on Nottingham Island knew nothing of American moonshot astronaut Neil Armstrong's "one big step for man, one giant leap for mankind." They heard about it some four months later. How could they not have heard? This was a radio station after all. Jean-Claude Rolland, an Algerian national who immigrated to Canada in 1962 and worked for the Department of Transport at Frobisher Island and later at Nottingham, recalls, "To stay sane and all together, we decided to completely break contact with the rest of the world. We did not listen to the radio. We just made our weather broadcasts and did maintenance. It was like Alcatraz." This is a strong comparison considering some have said Resolute Bay was far worse. Rolland explains, "we cut off contact to lessen the stress of separation from our families; otherwise the limited contact with the outside world would have just been a taunt and a pull. I'm sure even Amazonians knew there were men on the moon. We were among the few who didn't."

---

[59] *Marine Radio Communications in Canada*, Telecommunications & Electronics Branch (Ottawa: Department of Transport, 1968), p.10.

Arctic Region

Cape Hope's Advance

The Cape Hope's Advance radio station, with the call sign VAY, made its first broadcast on July 1, 1929. Cape Hope's Advance is located on the northwest point of the Ungava Peninsula, facing the Hudson Strait to the north. It is approximately 500 kilometres north of Kuujjuaq (Fort Chimo), a village of considerable size and the economic centre of Nunavik (Northern Québec). Quaqtaq, with a population today of approximately 300 inhabitants, was the closest settlement. In 1969, approaching its final year, the station itself had only single accommodations and meals were prepared by the station cook.

Winter operations at this station consisted of synoptic weather observations, both main and intermediate, which were compiled by a staff of two operators. During the summer, the station operated on a 24-hour basis and maintained a watch throughout the navigation season, which opened in July and carried on through October. Summertime brought radio traffic that consisted mainly of weather observations, ship-to-shore communications and administrative and private messages to and from the village, all relayed to Frobisher Bay via a point-to-point telegraphy circuit. Other stations such as Nottingham Island marine radio, Fort Chimo Aeradio and Clyde River Radio also communicated with Frobisher on the same circuit.

Communications between Cape Hope's Advance and Quaqtaq were carried out by canoe in summer and ski-doo in winter, both of which were government issued. Outside communications were provided by aircraft flying as part of the weekly mail and charter service. The Bell Telephone company also had a radio installation in Quaqtaq, and even the Québec provincial government had a radio service between its posts. Contact was limited, however, as the freeze-up period, which runs from October 1 to December 15, allowed no aircraft service except for mail. And as the plane approached—for example, over Nottingham Island— operators would step outside and look skyward, waving and impatiently waiting for the mailbag to drop.

In the early days, employees stayed at the station for 12 consecutive months. Relief personnel came only at the end of each summer. An icebreaker would leave Québec City with two operators and a cook on board en route for Cape Hope's Advance. In turn, the icebreaker brought back the employees who had completed their postings. The station had a relatively long life, closing its doors at the beginning of 1970, nearly a year before Nottingham Island closed. Now only two abandoned buildings remain at Cape Hope's Advance.

Two stations similar to Cape Hope's Advance—Chesterfield Inlet and Churchill—opened in 1928. The Chesterfield Inlet station had the call sign VBZ, and belonged to the Air Services group. The Churchill radio station, on the other hand, was operated for the purpose of shipping and its main purpose was to perform weather and ice observations, a service it provided until the end of the 1960s, when it closed. The stations came into being with the advent of a trade route to and from Churchill, Manitoba—a trade route that opened a frontier. The combination of railway and sea transport through the Hudson Strait proved more viable than the Great Lakes-Montréal route for the movement of grain. Nestled on the Hudson Bay coast, Churchill was deemed an ideal location to build a port. And by necessity, a radio station soon followed. Running from Le Pas to Churchill, the railway line that was eventually built was vital to the development of the eastern Arctic, bringing bulk supplies for trans-shipment by sea and by air.[60]

Iqaluit

Another station opened in the Canadian North in 1939. The installation at Frobisher Bay, now known as Iqaluit, was a combined aeradio and marine radio station offering a gamut of communications services, including point-to-point circuit telegraphy for the villages of Baffin Island. Frobisher Bay had long been regarded as a company town. The Canadian government owned all property at Iqaluit and provided all of the services and facilities.[61]

In September, 1957, Iqaluit found itself in the spotlight when the first commercial flight from San Francisco to Paris using the polar route landed there. Frobisher was deemed an excellent refuelling stop for trans-Polar flights between northern Europe and the American west coast. The base of Sondre Strom, Greenland, was formerly used as a service stop. During and after the Distant Early Warning (DEW) Line operations, which began in the 1950s, Iqaluit developed into a strategic central base for ferrying equipment and men to the radar line. In 1992, the DEW Line was replaced by more advanced detection equipment. Now the system is called the North Warning System.

---

[60] Michael Marsden, "Transportation in the Canadian North," William C. Wonders, *ed.*, *Studies in Canadian Geography* (Toronto: University of Toronto Press, 1972), p. 54.

[61] J. Roy Baxter, "The Old Bard Should Have Seen Us in the North!" *News on the DOT* (May-June 1963), p. 7.

Several aircraft are permanently stationed at Iqaluit to fly supplies to other airfields, weather and radio stations, mining prospectors and settlements in the Northwest Territories and Nunavik (Northern Québec). The base, located near the southern end of Baffin Island, was initially opened in 1942 by the United States as part of a chain of stations used to ferry planes to the United Kingdom. The Royal Canadian Air Force took over in 1946 and the U.S. again in 1952.[62] Iqaluit Coast Guard Radio was formed in 1985 by grouping the services of Killiniq, Resolute Bay, Coral Harbour and Frobisher Bay, all old marine radio stations closed earlier that year. A new building was opened in November, 1993.

Besides its strategic location, Baffin Island offers an ideal harbour for shipping. During the decades following the Second World War, tankers and freighters came in to unload yearly supplies in the break-up period of the summer months. The vast quantity of fuel needed for airlines was discharged by means of a floating pipeline in the bay. Storage tanks, holding approximately 13.6 million litres of oil were built by Shell and Imperial Oil.

Inuvik

In the north-west, the Royal Canadian Corps of Signals operated a summer station at Inuvik along the Mackenzie River. In 1923, the Canadian military established a wireless network extending from Edmonton to Aklavik, Northwest Territories—Aklavik being the closest outpost to Inuvik. Nineteen stations were constructed in all and the operations were maintained for the Department of Mines and Resources, the Bureau of Northwest Territories and Yukon Affairs. Aklavik soon became a household word when Albert Johnson, the mad trapper of Rat River, began preying on local trappers. The RCMP from Aklavik took charge of the matter but were not able to prevent the wounding of some radio personnel and RCMP officers, and the murder of one RCMP officer. It was not until Wop May, a famous Canadian aviator, got involved that the mad trapper was finally captured.

By the 1950s, air traffic in the Mackenzie area had increased significantly. In 1958, stations in the Yukon and the Northwest Territories radio system were taken over by the Department of Transport. Inuvik Canadian Coast Guard Radio came to be when services at the old Cambridge Bay facility were combined with those of the Inuvik station.

---

62 "Arctic Hub of Polar Route," *News on the DOT*, (December 1957), p. 5.

The government was by far the biggest employer in the North. Inevitably introducing sometimes traumatic modernization, the government brought the Inuit from stone-age economies to the jet-and-telecommunication age. However, the federal presence made, and continues to make, navigation reliable. The Department of Transport was the long-time coordinator of all freight moving into the eastern Arctic and the Archipelago and, through its Marine Operations Branch and the Canadian Coast Guard, it organized and performed annual sealifts. During the sealifts, Coast Guard icebreakers (all ready for survey and research, plus cargo capacity) accompanied chartered commercial and rate-per-ton vessels, usually from Québec, in a series of voyages that delivered heavy supplies to all accessible sites in the eastern Arctic.[63] Without this federal presence, perhaps the surviving crew members of the *Aigle D'Océan*, and many other mariners for that matter, would have perished.

Resolute

The exploration of regions inside the Arctic circle was largely due to the once legendary Northwest Passage. Roald Amundsen, with his ship *Gjoa*, staved off ice and peril for three years to complete the first passage to the west. He left Baffin Bay in August, 1903, and arrived at Nome, Alaska in July, 1906. Resolute Bay is located on Cornwallis Island, discovered by Captain W.E. Parry, yet another explorer on a quest to unveil the Northwest Passage. Resolute Bay got its name from the ship, HMS *Resolute*, assigned to the area for a research expedition in 1850-51.

It was not until the end of the Second World War that a telecommunications network was implemented for the express purpose of serving navigation. The plan, which proposed the construction of nine stations between 1947 and 1949, was accepted on February 12, 1946. In 1947, the project began and a meteorological and radio station went up at Resolute Bay. Two years later, the RCAF established a base with airport facilities. At this point, the Department of Transport confirmed its place in the North by assuming responsibilities for air and marine communications at Resolute Bay.

In the 1960s, an air-operational radioteletype circuit opened between Cambridge Bay and Resolute Bay (today, it is named Resolute). Later, VHF omni-range distance measuring equipment (VOR/DME) was

---

63 Michael Marsden, "Transportation in the Canadian North," Wonders, ed. *Studies in Canadian Geography* (Toronto: University of Toronto Press, 1972), p. 42.

installed at Whitehorse, Watson Lake, Yellowknife, Fort Simpson, Norman Wells, Inuvik, Cambridge Bay and Resolute. Cambridge Bay was the test facility for a new solid-state Arctic VOR/DME designed especially for the North. Before closing down completely, the busy time for radio operators at Resolute came in mid-July when an average of 10 to 15 vessels plied their way to the island by November. Now, a ship from the east coast for example, can go to Resolute up to five times in one season. In the early 1980s, commercial traffic rose a notable 40 percent. By 1984, radio communications with Resolute saw an increase of 43 percent. Resolute Coast Guard Radio is now officially closed; its final broadcast went out October 13, 1996. All of Resolute's services are now handled by the Iqaluit MCTS centre.

Some of the communications handled in the North may be from scientists visiting the high Arctic in the summer, usually for a few weeks at a time. They drill through the ice and get to the cores to figure out what the climate was like a thousand years ago. They sift through earth and stones looking for evidence of the Arctic when it was a subtropical land and discovering dinosaur bones, alligator teeth and the remains of creatures many millennia old. For them, radio is a means to stay in contact. Base managers keep communications schedules with all field camps. Voices blare in makeshift camps set up on tundra and ice.

Other visitors include thrill seekers such as Frenchman Stéphan Peyron who, in 1988, windsurfed from Resolute to the Magnetic North Pole, a distance of 1,500 kilometres. Like him, others flock to the North because of its intrinsic qualities.

Still, others are content to attempt to repeat the exploits of past explorers hungry for the route to the Orient. Claude Deschenes stands out from the many latter-day adventurers because he, unlike other thrill seekers, is a MCTS officer. Deschenes worked as a radio operator at Coast Guard stations and on Arctic re-supply vessels. About his voyages, Deschenes readily admits that he was like a "shoemaker with bad shoes," because his 10-metre, steel-hulled sloop, *Sedna II*, only had a very limited VHF radio capable of communicating within a range of only 30 to 50 kilometres. From his point of departure in Québec City, he took two months and two days to reach Resolute on Cornwallis Island. While in Resolute, he pondered the ice conditions that lay ahead.

Beginning in June, 1983, Deschenes followed the traditional route for sailing the Northwest Passage. He followed the coast of Greenland as far as Melville Bay before veering west to avoid the large pack ice between Greenland and Ellesmere Island. He continued on through Lancaster

Sound to Resolute, turning south into Peel Sound and following the coast to Ellesmere Island and Boothia Peninsula. From there, he sailed around the east coast of King William Island into Queen Maude Gulf, Coronation Gulf and finally into the Beaufort Sea. Deschenes wanted to make Point Barrow, Alaska, before mid-September. Once in the Pacific, Deschenes's intention was to head to San Francisco but, as of 1997, after three tries, he had still not completed the trip to the west.

Point-to-Point

Stations established by the government served an essential purpose by communicating with ships such as the historic *St. Roch*, which serviced many isolated posts and villages. But this was not the only kind of communications Canadian coast stations handled. They also provided communication services to small privately owned wireless stations at widely separated outposts. One such place was the mining centre of Ocean Falls, in northern British Columbia, which was connected to the outside world chiefly by means of point-to-point communications circuits.

On the Pacific coast alone, service was given to 36 stations located at canneries, pulp mills and mining towns, all otherwise nearly bereft of a link to the outside world. Where economic development existed, so too did radio. Whatever the role, be it aiding in rescue operations, helping ships and planes to stay their course or transmitting food orders, radio played an important role. As early as 1914, the communications services provided by the Le Pas and Port Nelson stations had already proven beneficial for the Department of Railways and Canals in a variety of construction projects. During the navigation season of 1914, a small 1/2 kW set and 600-metre wavelength enabled the Port Nelson station to also operate as a coast station. Later in the year, both stations handled a swell of 5,259 messages.

In more recent times, increasing resource explorations, shipping activities and the North's overall potential could not be overlooked. The successful Arctic Canada Traffic System (NORDREG Canada) was re-instituted in 1980 after a trial run the preceding year.[64] Operations at the NORDREG centre at Iqaluit were enhanced with the installation of a computer terminal that has access to a database of all information on ships plying Canadian waters. This allows MCTS officers to access the database to obtain, for example, information on marine traffic transiting regulated zones.

---

[64] Transport Canada Annual Report 1979/80, p.13.

Untin Bowler and Point-to-Point

In the late 1920s, expeditions having to do with the Canadian North gave point-to-point circuit telegraphy its place in the sun. For instance, the *Chicago Tribune* sponsored a pioneer course-charting flight to demonstrate the feasibility of air transportation between this continent and Europe. The flight was undertaken by the trimotored Sikorsky amphibian *Untin Bowler*.

The *Untin Bowler's* projected route was from Chicago via Cochrane, Ontario, Rupert House (Waskaganish), Port Burwell (Killiniq), Mount Evans and Greenland, to Berlin. Elaborate arrangements had been made for federal and provincial radio stations within range to maintain constant watch in order to assist the plane throughout its voyage. Special weather reports and forecasts were also prepared by the Dominion Meteorological Service, and transmitted to the plane by radio.

The *Untin Bowler* left Chicago on the morning of July 3, 1929, and arrived at Port Burwell early on July 9 after several stop-overs. On July 13, the plane was caught in an ice floe and swept to sea by a gale. It sank in the Hudson Strait. Fortunately there were no casualties and the crew was subsequently picked up by the CGS *Acadia* and taken to Port Churchill. Immediately following the incident, some 7,500 words of press traffic were handled by the Port Burwell coast station.

On a related matter, point-to-point also played an important role in the rescue of the members of the MacAlpine party, lost for two months after their two planes made forced landings at sea near Melbourne Island, within the Arctic Circle. The date was September 9, 1929. An aerial search tied in to the department's radio station at Ottawa, VAA, and Churchill, VAP, was launched. Radio stations of the Dominion Explorers at Stoney Rapids, Bathurst and Baker Lake joined the effort. The members of the MacAlpine party were found by Inuit on November 4, 1929. The news was instantly passed on to Cambridge Bay. From there, the *Baymaud*, a vessel owned by the Hudson's Bay Company, got hold of the news and transmitted it to the outside world from the ship's radio to the department's stations at Churchill and Ottawa.

Point-to-point communication was extensively used by public utilities and power companies, especially for emergency communications between power plants and distribution centres. The frequent interruption of the normal telegraph and telephone lines left companies with no other alternative. In the early 1930s, the British Columbia Telephone Company at Powell River looked to radio links to establish regular telephone service at isolated points. Sooner or later, though, many radio circuits were replaced by landline teletype circuits, due in great part to the expansion of vast landline networks belonging to wireless companies.

Archibald Fraser, Chief Engineer of the Radio Branch, was prophetic when he said, "Even in this age of wonders the rapid progress of radio stands out as phenomenal, and if we pause to consider its future possibilities, there is no doubt that intelligently employed, radio may become one of the most potent factors in bringing mutual understanding among all people as well as promoting an irresistible sentiment in favour of universal peace." Although quite ambitious in hindsight, the statement rings true. The field of communications has perhaps not brought universal peace but its hand in the long-standing tradition of safety is ever more present. In today's business context, communications enable the forging of ties with international partners to exploit space technology.

Major aspects of technology take their root in the early principles of radio. For instance, when the thermionic tube came out decades ago it was primarily used for radio and landline telephony and telegraphy. Thermionic devices consist of evacuated or plasma-filled cells in which electrons are boiled out of a hot cathode and collected at the cooler anode.[65] Today the same technology is a vital element in dozens of industries. "So tremendous will be the influence of the thermionic tube on the industry of tomorrow that the conception taxes even the fanciful imagination of a twentieth century Jules Verne." So said Archibald Fraser, again being somewhat prophetic.

Thermoelectric converters seem particularly well suited to work as an electrical power source for deep-space probes and other space vehicles. Heat for thermoelectric devices may come from solar, chemical or nuclear sources. What's more, thermoelectric technology includes low system weight and the ability to withstand acceleration greater than 30 times the force of gravity. This technology's high efficiency makes it a suitable energy source for low-power radio transmitters and other applications in remote and hostile terrestrial environments.[66]

Voice Broadcasts

Voice broadcasts first came to the North in the 1930s. Scheduled broadcasts began at Coppermine, Chesterfield Inlet and Port Churchill. Even the Royal Schooner *St. Roch* fell under this schedule. Prior to sailing on an extended voyage to the western Arctic, the RCMP auxiliary schooner was fitted with long- and short-wave transmitting and receiving equipment in order to maintain contact with its headquarters. An

---
65 Bellingham Antique Radio Museum web site.
66 Ibid.

operator from Marine and Fisheries was immediately assigned to the ship to operate the equipment. The broadcasts for both stations and ship consisted of press and personal messages.

Voice Broadcast Schedules

Coppermine,	VBK, 571 kHz	or	525 metres	11:05 p.m.	Wednesday & Saturday
Chesterfield Inlet,	VBZ, 555 kHz	or	540-5 metres	10:00 p.m.	Tuesday & Friday
Port Churchill,	VAP, 555 kHz	or	540-5 metres	11:00 p.m.	Monday & Thursday
St. Roch,	VGSR, 667 kHz	or	450 metres	11:00 p.m.	Wednesday & Saturday

Much later, in 1977, the development of voice broadcasts took a leap forward when a peripheral communication was established at Cape Dorset. The station was controlled from the Coral Harbour Coast Guard aeradio station via the Anik satellite. It was fully operational in time for the shipping season. Later, a marine telephone service using a link through the Anik satellite to the domestic telephone network was commissioned at the Killiniq Coast Guard radio station. The work was done to provide full, high-quality public correspondence to shipping in the Hudson Strait and the Labrador Sea.

Killiniq: Returning to the Old Haunts

Killiniq offered more than high-quality public correspondence. For George MacAlpine,[67] a radio operator from New Brunswick, the island was a sanctuary in the early 1970s. His life story seemed shrouded in myth. He took his leaves at Sable Island, a place steeped in the mix of fact and myth surrounding the island's many reported shipwrecks, a place where the ghosts of sailors secure their place in folklore. Similar stories are told of Killiniq. But even before setting foot on the northern island, MacAlpine had already shown signs of a singular nature. When stationed at Mont-Joli, he spent his off hours rambling along the railways carrying with him only a rucksack. Leading such a simple life, MacAlpine spent little of his earnings and, in fact, he amassed quite a respectable amount of money. He demonstrated no great regard for modern conveniences and accepted life with a rarely seen complacency.

Like many in his line of work, MacAlpine was asked to work up north. To him it was a viable option because he could capitalize on the northern living allowance, and it seems survival in the North is made easier with the very sort of temperament MacAlpine possessed. He visited

---

[67] No relation to the previously discussed MacAlpine party.

many areas in the province of Québec, but never found the peace that he finally did in the North.

Early explorers such as Henry Hudson sought, among other things, to penetrate the mysteries of the North, but instead met with death. Many former operators still talk of Uncle Henry's ghost. Some say he found neither rest nor peace since his death at the hands of a mutinous crew. Hudson's crew launched him and a few loyal officers in life rafts into the frigid waters of Hudson Bay. Was it Hudson's ghost who sent the cold chills through the Killiniq station, or an unsettling feeling that gripped the operators as they sent out their weather broadcasts?

It is fitting that MacAlpine found, at Killiniq, a sanctuary. Years before, he was at Resolution Island, one of several islands dotting the Eastern Arctic. But it is at Killiniq that MacAlpine's presence is most remembered. In 1975, MacAlpine apparently died in his quarters of cerebral hemorrhaging. He was found, clothes soiled with bile, by the Latvian cook who called Heli-Québec in Fort Chimo on the HF frequency to inform the company of a body to be evacuated. Unfortunately, helicopters and planes did not often visit such remote quarters, given that the Killiniq station is a 375-kilometre trek from Fort Chimo (Kuujjuaq) through a region frequently plagued by severe storms. Aircraft were often grounded days at a time. The question of what to do with the body before the helicopter arrived quickly became a pertinent issue. Well-meaning government employees thought of freezing him sitting down on the roof of a shed in order to place the body in the passenger seat of the helicopter pilot. Peter Horsman of Heli-Québec, the pilot who flew the body out, asked if rigor mortis had set in. Indeed it had, and the unfortunate passenger was taken out in a lying position. But not before the RCMP officer who accompanied the pilot ruled that the operator had indeed died of natural causes.

All the while, MacAlpine's sister communicated with the station many times to verify when the body was to arrive. She had been in a hurry to receive the remains of the departed to obtain the death certificate and to settle his estate.

Normally, at the end of each sailing season, few of the personnel remained on the island—to wit, the cook and a sole operator. The staff was reduced due to little or no navigation in the northern waters. And of course, George MacAlpine typically volunteered to stay for winter. Radio operators Martin Grégoire and Jean-Pierre Lehnert were among those who headed south. MacAlpine's work consisted of performing synoptic meteorological observations every six hours, and assuring emergency and administrative communications for the local village of Killiniq, numbering slightly more than 100 inhabitants at the time. The communications links were ensured with Frobisher (Iqaluit), VFF, via radiotelegraph. Who, though, would replace MacAlpine now? Jean-Pierre Lehnert, a radio operator at the time, remembers.

> There I was somewhere between Christmas and New Year's on the ice-pack in Fort Chimo wondering what on earth I was doing here. While a month or so passed, I thought about the bizarre stories I had heard concerning the inhabitants of this distant place. The worst one by far was told to me by my superiors; I was going to Killiniq to relieve a cadaver.

Without further delay, Lehnert was sent to Killiniq to replace MacAlpine. MacAlpine's body was eventually flown back to his home in New Brunswick, leaving Lehnert in charge of the station.

> The next days I spent gathering the things of the recently departed and avoiding the macabre feelings that tend to creep up on you in such circumstances—my assigned quarters were George's quarters. But it wasn't just the sleeping quarters, there was a particular atmosphere in the station itself. And the best way to describe it is "haunted." The station had previously been an Inuit dwelling, and with no real existing upkeep, the building soon became little more than livable. An old dwelling, that's all the housing committee had been able to provide despite the government's generous lease agreement.
>
> When I entered the first time, nothing had so much as moved since George's last watch. I noticed the pallet he had made for himself in the station. George once said he hated walking to the station at night because he met people on the way. So he slept at the station. When I set down to work I would hurry through it because I didn't want to prolong my stay there.

Apparently, MacAlpine had not been the shrewdest administrator. Lehnert and others often found themselves throwing scathing remarks at him for falling behind in paperwork, at times months overdue. But when Lehnert was alone in the station and in the clutches of an ill sensation, he found himself apologizing for past remarks.

During the whole length of Lehnert's stay at the station, he never once entered the room where MacAlpine died, except to gather George's belongings. "The whole story seems absurd now," says Lehnert, "but I wonder how anybody else would have reacted in such circumstances." Even more strange was MacAlpine's dog, who left MacAlpine a week before he died. Before the dog left, it would cower on the ground, motionless, seemingly guessing his master's end. MacAlpine had apparently called Keeta many times but his cries remained unanswered. Later, after the alleged omen seemingly became a reality, Lehnert called out for the dog and it appeared suddenly, its tail wagging vigorously, suggesting, perhaps, a more positive omen. "I gladly accepted the prophecy that I had more than a week to live," Lehnert admits.

Besides what appeared to him to be a discomforting presence at the time, Lehnert had other encumbrances to shrug off. Undeniably the station was in a bad state. He overlooked a broken door, which remained forever ajar, permitting the whipping wind and snow to enter. The windows had their panes taped over with masking tape to prevent the outflow of heat. As well, he overlooked the heater breaking down occasionally. In coat and boots, he worked his shifts, at times dusting off an outdated copy of *Radio Aids to Marine Navigation*; recent publications were nowhere to be found.

The console, which had been installed by the Canadian Marconi Company, was also less than adequately functional. For instance, to work the marine LF and HF frequencies and point-to-point simultaneously, operators had to sport three different pairs of headphones and operate two press-to-talk switches. The LF marine Elekstrisk transmitter, built in Norway, was shipboard equipment that required tedious adjustments every time a frequency change was in order. Given the make of the transmitter, parts were undoubtedly hard to come by. At the time, the receivers were from ITT Mackay and did not allow for band scanning. As for the meteorological desk, it was made of trimmed planks of plywood (for the simple reason that the usual metal parts had been forgotten at Resolution Island).

Furthermore, at a time when most government stations still offered services to both aircraft and vessels, Killiniq had no radio beacon for local flights into the village. Operators had little choice but to transmit, for hours, on the marine frequency of 484 kilohertz for direction-finding purposes. Even more tedious was the 5,810-kilohertz point-to-point frequency which, as it turned out, was the only option for broadcasting weather conditions to pilots.

Still more indication of the dilapidated conditions at Killiniq were the complaints from local Inuit elders that the bottom portion of the fence around the receiving and transmitting antennae rose half a metre above the ground in some places. Curious wandering children could easily crawl under the fence to gain access to the dangerous compound. The problem, according to Lehnert, was hard to fix when tools were nowhere to be found.

Understandably, some operators may have found a posting of six months at Killiniq quite sufficient. Add to this the gradual introduction of new technology, which at times became unsettling, and the overall situation at Killiniq seems more an exercise in exacerbated alienation than an exciting stint in a rugged, natural environment.

But MacAlpine seemed to thrive on the isolation. He was unlike other operators in that he enjoyed an almost obsessive solitude. The times called for no overstepping of personal space, and MacAlpine would have been the last to do such a thing. With his pallet set up in a closed corner of the station, little friction could be anticipated from George MacAlpine. His life, to some, is the source of many varying stories, and his death as a hermit gave rise to more.

In 1978, three years after MacAlpine's death, both the air and marine sides of the Telecommunications Branch became separate, independent bodies, meaning the Killiniq station fell under the authority of the Canadian Coast Guard.

Despite his feelings of unease, Lehnert returned to Killiniq to close the station in 1985, a decade after his first purported encounters with the ghosts. From that point on, Killiniq's operations were remotely controlled from the Iqaluit MCTS centre. With no one to operate the Killiniq site directly from the island, some believe that Killiniq may still somehow be inhabited by one operator—MacAlpine.

The project to remotely control the Killiniq site from Iqaluit was indeed a new frontier for engineers and electronic technicians. Denis Tardif, Technical Services, was in charge of the project which centralized all the installations. To this end, four trailers were brought to the site— one housed the generators; one contained electrical equipment; another held the Telesat Canada equipment; and the fourth afforded temporary shelter for technicians. Four 13,638-litre reservoirs and one helicopter pad completed the overhaul of the station-cum-peripheral site. Emphasis was placed on reliable electronic equipment. For instance, double remote equipment, double local and supply regulators, double supply batteries, a sophisticated satellite link interface, new receivers, transmitters and antennae, a reliable alarm system and an emergency radio installation were all part of this transformation.

Later, an automated and autonomous system of troubleshooting was installed, allowing a technician at Iqaluit to measure the sensitivity of the receivers or even assess the reliability of the antennae at Killiniq.

Chapter 6

The Pacific Region

The subject of marine radio communications is no longer the focus of reporters; nor is it the lure it once was for young men in search of a pioneering career. Even ocean-going vessels, once employers of numerous radio operators, now look to the sky for communications.

Like the advent of the telegraph, the coming of wireless compressed the time of communication from days to fractions of a second. Wireless was a technological revolution. For example, in February, 1795, the *Kentucky Gazette* ran an article about Alexander Mackenzie reaching the Pacific,[68] a feat he had accomplished in 1793. Why was such a monumental achievement reported so much later? The reasons are unclear. But one thing is certain, communication then was measured in increments of days, and the time between sending and receiving varied according to mode of transportation used, be it canoe, the short-lived pony express, train or ocean-going vessel.

In the 1840s, Samuel Morse's telegraph line running from Washington to Baltimore began the communication revolution. Later, in 1865, the California State Telegraph Company extended its service north to New Westminster, British Columbia. On April 18, 1865, the line was ready to handle communications.[69] One of the first messages on the west-coast line announced the assassination of Abraham Lincoln. As more and more telegraph lines were set up across the landscapes of North America and Europe, societies witnessed the compression of time. News came faster as decisions were made quicker.

---

[68] Henry Nash Smith, *Virgin Land, The American West as Symbol and Myth* (Cambridge, MA: Harvard University Press, 1978), p.20.

[69] Larry Reid, *The Story of the West Coast Radio Service* (Vancouver: Chameleon Publishing and Graphic Design, 1992), p.87.

Marconi Loses the "Shoe-in"

Marconi was making great strides with his wireless stations on the east coast and later on the Great Lakes. Certainly, around 1907, radio was rapidly becoming an important aid to shipping. Up-to-date press releases had already become a boon for passengers travelling on the St. Lawrence, as marine radio was burgeoning into a media tool. Shipping companies were urging the Canadian government to establish radio stations on the British Columbia coast. But what really sparked the creation of a chain of radio stations in the Pacific region was the sinking of the American steamer *Valenchia* off the coast of Vancouver Island and the loss of lives.

Relief for distressed sailors in the Pacific coastal waters had generally been provided by rescue huts built along what is now known as the west-coast line. The huts were built at regular intervals and were stocked with blankets, medical kits and emergency food stores. More importantly, each rescue hut had a magneto telephone with instructions written in several languages explaining how to call for assistance. The telephone line linking the huts with the mainland was patrolled regularly by linemen who both repaired breaks caused by windfalls and responded to emergency calls to assist shipwrecked sailors.[70]

Larry Reid, a retired District Manager of Pacific Region and author, said this about the west-coast line: "In theory, it was a good idea; but in practice, it failed on one important count. The galvanized wire had been strung from tree to tree along the trail. Falling trees broke the line, putting it out of service—particularly in stormy weather when it was most needed. The rescue huts, despite the breaks in the lines were quite valuable, but could only complement a more immediate means to provide safety."

The history of wireless on the Canadian west coast differs from the east-coast story, largely because of one important detail: Marconi's services were not retained to set up the wireless chain and it was installed instead by government employees from Ottawa. The government decided to go with the Shoemaker system because its promoters outbid all other competitors, especially Marconi. The Marconi Company was pushed aside because it had yet to accept the principle of interstation communication—that is, communicating with any ship regardless of system used. Many vessels plying Pacific waters were already using the Massie system.[71]

---

[70] Ibid., p. 90.

[71] Department of Marine and Fisheries Annual Report, 1908, p. 96. Walter Massie, an early radio experimenter, founded the Massie Wireless Telegraph Company in 1905. His company established New England's coastal stations. The Marconi Company bought the U.S. Wireless Telegraph company in 1912, which had just purchased Massie's company.

The Shoemaker system was unquestionably more up to date than the one being used in the Gulf of St. Lawrence. It was also less expensive to operate and, according to the figures quoted by the Marconi Company, to maintain. Without a doubt, the government's decision concerning the west-coast communications was a blow to the monopolistic Marconi Company.

Marconi's aims were again thwarted when the government granted a licence to the competing Dominion De Forest Wireless Telegraph Company to construct an experimental station at Cap-aux-Meules in Québec's Magdalen Islands.

As well, in 1907, the government took absolute control of the wireless service on board all government vessels. From the onset of wireless communications, service had been provided by the Marconi Company. The company's operators did not consider themselves subject to ship discipline, undeniably interfering with the service itself—yet another blow suffered by the Marconi Company.[72] Given the benefit of hindsight, Marconi's earlier stronghold on wireless communications can now be compared to the Sony Betamax / VHS phenomenon. Not unlike Sony, Marconi lost considerable momentum because, as well as refusing non-Marconi communications, he was reticent to sell patent rights. Sony tried to maintain a technical monopoly; so, too, did Marconi. With that in mind, the Department of Marine and Fisheries was wary of non-competitive price control. In 1907, government authorities arrived on the coast to select the following sites:

- Gonzales Hill for the Victoria station;
- The high bluff at Point Grey for the Vancouver station;
- The most eastern point of Vancouver Island, jutting out into the Strait of Georgia, for the Cape Lazo station; and,
- Pachena and Estevan Points for the west coast of the island, both of which already had lighthouses.

By 1909, the Pacific coast group of stations counted three operational stations—Point Grey, VAI, Victoria, VSD, and Pachena Point, KPD, later to become VAD. Operators at sea and on shore exchanged weather reports consisting of cloud conditions, approximate strength and direction of winds, barometer and temperature readings, and sea conditions, at least three times a day. Ships were not charged in the early months of the service, but the first year reaped $500, all collected from commercial traffic.

---

72 Col. F. Gaudreau, Deputy Minister of Marine and Fisheries, *Marine and Fisheries Annual Report*, 1907 (Ottawa: October 22, 1907), p. 95.

The equipment at Pachena, however, had many shortcomings at the time, especially the 1.5-kilowatt spark set, which was hopelessly inadequate for the job operators had to do. For instance, in order to transmit a message to Victoria, a distance of only about 125 kilometres, the operator had to relay it through a U.S. station at Cape Flattery, a peninsula jutting out into the Strait of Juan de Fuca. The arrangement complicated matters in that American operators communicated with the American Morse code as opposed to the International code. This problem remained until communications were eventually standardized in the new regulations imposed following the sinking of the *Titanic*.

C.P. Edwards, Controller for the Government Radio Service and also a former Marconi employee, came to the west coast in 1909 to inspect the existing stations and to supervise the construction of three more stations: Digby Island (Prince Rupert), Triangle Island and Ikeda Head on the Queen Charlotte Islands. There was somewhat of a rush to complete the system because at that particular time, demand for marine radio communications was on the rise. The CPR Empress Ships, the Canadian-Australian passenger vessels, British Columbia coastwise vessels and the G.T.P. passenger ships were all equipping with radio. Ship owners opted for wireless because of the lower insurance rates, safety and the fuel economy resulting from precise bearings.

With the ever-increasing expansion of wireless, ship captains no longer had to rely totally on "shooting the sun," "dead reckoning" or lead lines. A new navigation pattern was set—captains approaching land could already obtain accurate reports of their ship's position via a multitude of radio stations. A parallel expansion had already taken place just a few years before on the American west coast. The United Wireless Company of America built stations at Seattle, Astoria, San Francisco, Ketchikan and later at Cape Flattery. The American network extended as far south as San Diego on the Mexican border. When the Prince Rupert station opened in 1911, it marked the completion of a chain of communication extending from Vancouver, on the southern mainland, to northern British Columbia. A cable from Digby Island to the mainland was laid and a landline was strung along the Grand Trunk poles to the city of Prince Rupert. Before the first war, the province of British Columbia had full communications coverage of its coast. The chain of stations provided the only means of communication with the Queen Charlotte Islands, and offered communications services to commercial stations opened by owners of lumber camps, canneries and paper mills.

Prince Rupert marine radio covered the entrance to Prince Rupert Harbour, as well as the waters surrounding Digby Island. On January 8, 1924, a portion of the quarantine wharf collapsed during a heavy gale, thus severing the telegraph cable to Prince Rupert. The cable was beyond repair. Temporary wireless communications were established with Prince Rupert by installing small tube equipment in the Prince Rupert Post Office building in town. The station would remain at Digby Island until 1967 when its services were combined with those of Prince Rupert aeradio. In 1981, marine communications were moved to Seal Cove.

Like many other communications and traffic centres across the country, the Prince Rupert centre saw the integration of radio and Vessel Traffic Services in 1996. New console configurations were drawn up and installed, making multi-task radio/VTS operations a reality. The Prince Rupert MCTS centre now controls communications sites at Sandspit, Hunter Point, Barry Inlet, Rose Inlet, Cumshewa, Dundas Island, Kitimat, Klemtu, Mount Dent, Mount Gil, Mount Hays, Naden Harbour and Van Inlet.

The First Decade

Like early American stations, the Canadian west-coast stations were combined operating/dwelling facilities. Often the operations room was at one end of the station and the living quarters at the other. The annexed dwelling, former wireless operator Jack Bowerman remarked, "somewhat suggests that original planners had a dim view of the future of radio,"[73] for soon radio outgrew its expected purpose and separate dwellings were built. The Pacific coast stations saw their communications increase by 50 percent in just one year after the second year of operation. The expansion continued when, in 1911, the Superintendent, decided to maintain 24-hour watches at all stations. This, in turn, brought more operators into the service.

With the introduction of night watches, operators found that the communications range of stations increased by as much as 500 percent—in fall, winter and spring. Even at that early stage, the longest distance reached was from Triangle Island to Honolulu, some 4,000 kilometres.

---

[73] Jack Bowerman, a wireless operator who later became Radio Inspector, wrote an unpublished manuscript entitled *Early History of the Government Wireless Service on the British Columbia Coast*, circa 1950.

While increased range of night-time communications was true for most stations, contact between Pachena Point and Victoria—separated by only 125 kilometres—remained impossible, day or night.

The 1912 London Radiotelegraph Conference and the SOLAS Conference, two years later, decreed radio equipment mandatory on most ships. As a direct result, radio's value was confirmed. However, an ensuing shortage of operators was felt throughout the network, especially on the Pacific coast. The "Learners' Division" was created for on-the-job training. Junior operators went without pay until they could pass the learners' examination. They were tested on their knowledge of the equipment and were expected to be proficient in International Morse code, sending and receiving at a rate of at least 15 words per minute. From the junior position, operators progressively moved on to third, second and finally first operator status. By 1918, 493 employees were working for the Radiotelegraph Service.

In addition to the International code, wireless operators had to know the American Morse code, as a considerable amount of commercial traffic was transmitted in the early decades via the telegraph system. Most coast stations had a link to commercial landlines. Operating the telegraph lines with their required knowledge of the American code posed only a minor problem, because most Canadian operators were ex-British Post Office telegraphists who had come to British Columbia during the immigration boom of 1910.

Not all landline operators crossed over to the west-coast radio service. And it was not because they had to learn the International Morse code—a hurdle for some—but rather a question of money. Government jobs paled in comparison to the moderately higher wages, town postings and better working schedules offered by commercial telegraph companies. For example, government operators at the very beginning earned $2.25 a day during the probation period and $65 a month as a starting third operator. Promotions to second and first operator brought a $5 increase with each progression. In these early days, because of the popularity of radio, promotion was indeed fairly rapid.

Earlier, in 1910, supervisors had decided that only married men should be hired as operators. The rule was followed under the assumption that government property and the service itself would greatly benefit. A single man already posted at a station had to commit to marry within a year. But after sifting fact from fiction, supervisors soon found that it was difficult to get married staff to work at remote locations. The questionable rule was eventually abolished, and single men continued to work at both the remote and the more favourably located sites.

There was not much traffic to handle in the beginning years of the west-coast service. The industry standard for radio technology at the time was a magnetic detector allowing the limited range of 150 to 350 nautical miles (278 to 648 km). Because of the relative newness and undeniable fickleness of this budding technology, CPR ferry boats running between Vancouver and Victoria would lose touch with Point Grey about three quarters of the way to Victoria, resulting in a brief lag before establishing contact with Victoria. Not long after, a temporary procedure was found to circumvent the inconvenience. The government telegraph service had a phone circuit from Bamfield to Victoria with a tie-in at both the Pachena and Victoria radio stations. When the telegraph offices closed in the evening, the operators patched these two stations into this circuit, giving Pachena a direct phone link with Victoria at night.[74] Equipment upgrades eventually eliminated the lags in communication.

The normal working wavelengths were around 300, 600 and 1,500 metres. The 600-metre (or 500-kilohertz) band was used for distress communications. Frequency control was still in its infancy, and operators could only tune aerials with fairly high "Q" tuned circuits comprising inductance and large capacitors.[75] The capacitors were made of copper plates with sheets of glass serving as a dielectric. The old, oversized equipment was later replaced with oil-filled capacitors. When operators wished to change frequencies on the old equipment, a walk to the transmitter room was necessary in order to change taps (movable connections) on the aerial inductance. Longer wavelengths were tried and the Shoemaker glass tubular type condensers were eventually replaced with the Marconi oil dielectric condensers. This equipment upgrade meant an improved signal between Pachena and Victoria, thereby making it possible for a direct wireless link between the two stations where none had been available before.

In general, the spark transmitters and crystal receivers were very crude but seldom failed. The six-horsepower Fairbanks Morse engines gave little trouble, other than requiring ignition system replacements every few weeks, and these gas engines were run only when charging the batteries or when the transmitter was in use. When operators received a call, they had to go into the engine room to start the engine before they could transmit a reply. Since coast-station operators encountered regular problems with the ignition system, the reply was often delayed. Ship operators, of course, were well aware of this and would patiently wait.

---

[74] Ibid.
[75] Ibid.

Triangle Island

Triangle Island is 64 kilometres north-west of Cape Scott, at the northern tip of Vancouver Island. It has been described as a cone-shaped rock 207 metres high and approximately five kilometres in circumference. Triangle Island is bereft of trees and has poor soil, allowing only for the growth of wind-stunted crab apple bushes, salal and coarse grass, and no doubt offering little protection from the elements. Added to this limited landscape were the aerial masts made from tall trees brought over from the mainland. After completely peeling off the bark, the structure was shaped by hand using a large drawknife. The masts were then elevated with gin poles, blocks and tackle and a small hand windlass.[76]

On October 22, 1912, a severe windstorm with 160-kilometre-per-hour gales was recorded, breaking the anemometer as well as the shaft holding the four rotating cups at the Triangle Island station. Gale-force winds were commonplace on the island but conditions were more severe that October day: chimneys toppled, and the island's lone office building moved off its foundation. Luckily, the two large water-cooling tanks in the engine room held the office secure to the ground and, unlike the masts, the offices did not fall into the sea. Strung along the path between the station and the sleeping quarters, a rope was fastened on poles to help operators walk upright in the wind. As one might imagine, the station was often out of service. But a temporary aerial was eventually rigged on the roof, putting it back on the air shortly after the storm of 1912.

Later that year, the Department of Marine and Fisheries undertook to wedge heavy 8"x 8" shores against the sides of the buildings at Triangle Island, steel cables were secured over the roofs and workers made fast to cement deadmen in the ground.

Government reports show that Triangle Island had a range of 300 nautical miles (556 km)—it was hoped that the station would work long-distance communications. However, Estevan Point, which was reported to have a range of only 150 nautical miles (278 km), was considered a better station for long-distance communications with ships, and eventually the west-coast station was upgraded accordingly.

Triangle Island covered the Inside Passage between Seymour Narrow and Millbank Sound until the opening of the Alert Bay station in 1913. From then on, Triangle Island acted only as a relay station for the north/south traffic, maintaining a watch for deep-sea and coastwise ships, and handling traffic for the Queen Charlotte Island stations, Ikeda Head and Dead Tree Point.

---

[76] Ibid.

Alert Bay eliminated many of the dead spots the ship operators encountered when navigating in the Inside Passage. The main transmitting apparatus at Alert Bay was a five-kilowatt, 240-cycle synchronous disc transmitter, belt-connected to a 10-horsepower Canadian Fairbanks Morse gasoline engine. The backup set was a two-kilowatt synchronous disc, 120-cycle transmitter, belt-driven by a six-horsepower engine. The transmitter, built in the Esquimalt workshop just outside Victoria, worked well compared to other brand names. The workshop was opened in the Esquimalt dockyard to conduct tests. An experimental test room housed a 10-horsepower three-phase motor and two transformers.

Aerial technology steadily improved in the early decades, not unlike receivers which became increasingly more selective in tuning with each passing year. The reception range, however, remained limited to the sensitivity of the crystal detector.

From 1911 on, and for many years, most of the radio equipment in Canadian ships and coast stations was Marconi brand equipment. The Government Service and the Canadian Marconi Company worked in close cooperation, and many Marconi employees transferred to the government for the opportunity to work ashore. After the sinking of the *Titanic* and the subsequent international conferences, Marconi was compelled to accept the principle of interstation communication. In doing so, the Marconi Company re-gained its lagging momentum.

In 1919, the Triangle Island site was closed due to constant and restrictive rebuilding costs, which took their toll on the District Superintendent's budget. To find another site for the Triangle Island station, two departmental employees conducted tests in the Port Hardy-Shushartie-Bull Harbour areas of Hope Island using a 10" spark coil and a crystal detector receiver, and finally choosing Bull Harbour as the most suitable site.

Bull Harbour and Comox

The Bull Harbour station opened in 1921 and, from the onset and as a result of the escalating ship traffic in the area, became a very busy relay station. Bull Harbour is located on a narrow neck of land separating the harbour from the wide-open Pacific near the north-east tip of Vancouver Island. The stretch of open water between Shushartie, a nearby village, and Bull Harbour was often a perilous crossing during storms—at times so much so that operators, scheduled to work at the station, stayed at Shushartie overnight. To make matters worse, Shushartie had no dock for boarding or landing passengers. Only a float, placed in the middle of the bay, allowed steamers to approach. A rowboat or smaller craft bridged the remaining distance.

Similar problems faced Pachena Point and Estevan Point. For example, at Estevan, CPR steamers landed or picked up passengers in Hesquiat Harbour because shallow water prevented ships from coming closer to shore. In severe weather, captains sometimes even refused that approach. In good weather though, Hesquiat natives went out to meet passengers in a canoe.

Around this time, in the early 1920s, the 10 stations on the Pacific coast were divided into two groups—one to handle ship-to-shore communications and the other to offer interstation or ordinary telegraphic service. The split was essential to preserve the efficiency of ship-to-shore service, as it was becoming seriously congested with ordinary telegraphic business. Under this program, the station at Ikeda Head was closed in September, 1920, and its equipment transferred to Bull Harbour. The low-power station at Pachena Point was temporarily closed because of its redundance under the new scheme. The two stations had been operating since 1908, but the greatly increased range of modern ship sets permitted the closings without minimizing service.

In 1908, a station opened on a high sandstone bluff known as Cape Lazo. The call sign was SKD, but in 1913 it was changed to VAC. Initially, the station had a range of 250 kilometres. Not unlike most stations in the west-coast network, the power supply at Cape Lazo was generated by a five-horsepower gas engine. For nearly six decades, the station broadcast mainly weather reports to ships plying the Strait of Georgia. Then, in October 1962, its operations were transferred to the Comox municipal airport.

Construction of the present Comox centre began at the original wireless station site in October, 1991. It was not until February, 1993, that CGRS operations began at the building on Wireless Road. Since that time, Comox has increased its coverage area by including the peripheral sites of Calvert Island, Holberg, Port Hardy, Alert Bay and Texada Island. Other communication sites are at Discovery, Cape Lazo, Holberg and Comox.

For its part, Pachena Point had seen a significant reduction in its workload and was finally closed in 1922 only to be reopened shortly after as a direction-finding station. The U.S. government had already established direction-finding stations on the Washington coast, and a station on the south-west coast of Vancouver Island was urgently needed to tie in with the

American stations which were overburdened with the ship traffic entering the Strait of Juan de Fuca.[77]

The government allotted $2,000 to overhaul the Pachena station of which $1,200 was spent on a Canadian Marconi direction-finding receiver. In 1922, the Pachena direction-finding station opened and, within a short while, was averaging 300 bearings a month. The station used the Bellini-Tossi principle of fixed loops and goniometer. Ship captains, however, seemed reticent to rely on the new technology at first. The same held true with the later implementation of vessel traffic services on Vancouver Island. The prejudice against direction finding soon diminished and an average of 300 bearings a month were given the first year of operation at Pachena Point, essentially spelling the end of "dead reckoning."

The End of Dead Reckoning

The decade and a half following Marconi's much-vaunted reception of the letter "S" saw radio technology jump from spark communications to continuous wave, all triggered by the three-element vacuum tube. The triode vacuum tube was invented in 1906, but developed slowly and only became popular during World War I. Before this, spark transmitters produced discontinuous radio waves which were very broadly tuned at best. Receivers were arrayed with a variety of detectors, but no electronic amplification. Following the advent of tube technology, radio transmitters produced a continuous carrier wave with an assigned frequency or wavelength. These new tube transmitters could easily transmit on high frequencies as well as on low frequencies. Also, with the coming of the tube, voice transmission became possible and receivers could amplify weak signals to loudspeaker volume. These new receivers were capable of sharp tuning (selectivity or separation of received signals according to carrier frequency), thus cutting down on interference.

Direction finders were sprouting up everywhere around the world except, curiously, in Germany. During the First World War, it became obvious that the Allied Forces had the upper hand over the Germans in this respect—a situation that became clearly apparent in the Battle of Jutland. The new direction-finding equipment was set up in a group of stations along the south-east coast of England. From here, the Royal Navy was not only able to determine the position of any German ship

---

[77] The first direction-finding station in Canada opened in 1917, at Chebucto Head, in the approaches to Halifax Harbour.

that left harbour, but could accurately track its course across the North Sea. The Germans were using their wireless systems and therefore had to take special precautions wherever direction-finding stations kept vigil—any communication could have betrayed their presence and position.[78]

In later years, the popularity of similar direction-finding equipment installed on ships grew significantly. Captains were able to obtain their own bearings from known land radio-beacon stations and, in turn, the use of land direction-finding stations seriously declined. Twenty years after it first opened, and like many other direction-finding stations across Canada, the Pachena facility closed and was converted into a powerful radio beacon site. Today, the Tofino MCTS centre, located at Amphitrite Point on the west coast of Vancouver Island, is basically the result of the growth of the old Pachena Point and Estevan Point stations. The Tofino coast station originally opened in 1971 after the separation of air and marine services. Together, the services had been offered from the Tofino Airport since 1956. The year 1956 commemorates the closing of both the Estevan Point and Pachena Point stations, the services of which were combined at the Tofino Airport. The Tofino MCTS centre currently controls communications sites at Eliza Dome, Mount Ozzard, Port Alberni, Estevan Point, Esperanza and Nootka.

The Estevan Point installation was improved for greater range, enabling longer distances for transpacific ship communications. A new powerhouse was built. A large storage capacity battery was brought in, and a 50-horsepower semi-diesel Fairbanks Morse engine and a Navy 15-kilowatt spark transmitter were installed. By 1916, Estevan Point boasted a range of 500 nautical miles (833 kilometres).

Constant technological upgrading brought the Estevan Point coast station a good degree of prominence. During the night watch, operators contacted ships in all parts of the Pacific, with the aim of obtaining their positions. Eventually, the daily morning report of ship contacts became more and more lengthy. The contacts reached surprising distances, considering the otherwise limited spark equipment being used.

In November, 1924, nightly contact was maintained with the *S.S. Tahiti* during its entire run from San Francisco to New Zealand—the final contact reached 5,500 miles, just before the ship docked at Auckland. What's more, in January, 1925, a similar communication was

---

[78] Sharon A. Babaian, *Radio Communication in Canada: An Historical and Technological Survey*, p. 28.

maintained with the *S.S. Makura* on its way to Australia; the last communication sent originated 6,057 miles from Vancouver.[79]

Both of these ships usually transmitted on designated wavelengths, although some operators admitted that the *Makura* and the *Tahiti* selected slightly longer wavelengths when sending their position. The reasoning was simple: they steered clear of the interference created by other stations and thunderstorms by transmitting on 450 metres. By the same token, Estevan Point operators transmitted on an irregular wavelength (1,100 metres) a wavelength normally used to transmit nightly news reports.

These spectacular communications were achieved with rather crude equipment. Jack Bowerman, a former operator, said that it was almost as easy to contact ships at great distances with the one-kilowatt and five-kilowatt spark transmitters as it was with the newer and more powerful Type I transmitter.[80] This raises the question of solar radiation, which varies according to the so-called 11-year sunspot cycle. This cycle, it was discovered, affects the quality of radio communications due to increases or reductions in radiation emitted from the sun. On one hand, the ionosphere can bounce a low-frequency (LF) signal over 8,000 kilometres away, while a receiver three kilometres from the transmitting site will not pick it up. But by contrast, the sunspot cycle can have the effect of suppressing a signal to just a few kilometres. The same holds true for today's very high frequency (VHF) signals; fluctuations in the ionosphere can change the usual 50-kilometre range of a VHF signal to 500 kilometres.

By all accounts, the *Tahiti* and *Makura* communications received considerable media attention in Australia. The intercontinental communications confirmed what was already in the works: the Department of Marine and Fisheries had, two years earlier, granted licences to the Canadian Marconi Company to build super-high power long-distance communications stations at Montréal and Vancouver.

The construction of the two stations was tied to the Imperial Chain which, despite many deadlocks, finally received approval by several Commonwealth countries. The Vancouver station was to communicate with Australia, while the Montréal station was to communicate with Europe, under the Commonwealth plan. The cost of these short-wave

---

[79] Jack Bowerman, *Early History of the Government Wireless Service on the British Columbia Coast*.

[80] In 1924, the Department of Marine and Fisheries installed continuous wave transmitters at Gonzales Hill, Estevan Point, Alert Bay and Digby Island.

stations is estimated to have been $300,000 each. For some clients, communications remained poor. Coastwise steamers complained that it was difficult to raise the inside stations due to interstation traffic. Later, a listening period was scheduled every half hour on 600 metres for the inside stations.

Radio Broadcasting

In 1920, the first broadcast station went on air.[81] That station was XWA (later CFCF Montréal). Marconi owned and operated the station, the call letters for which are still being used today by one of Montréal's English-language television broadcasters. The company began its broadcasts, once a week, in December, 1920, transmitting on the 1,100-metre wavelength. However, the Marconi claim to "first broadcast" was challenged by Westinghouse in Pittsburgh. No matter whose claim is correct, Canada remains well at the front of the telecommunications pioneering line.

It seems that the seductive power of radio was strong enough in 1920 that scam artists at the time had little difficulty swindling some less discerning people.

> Nanaimo B.C. August 14, 1920
> Dear Sirs,
> I seen in the paper were the Lazo Wireless are to be sold out now, about 10 years ago I put $1,050 in that Company but I had not a line from them since they got my money, now I wonder if you could find out something about it for me.
> Mrs. E.E. Bauer thanking you very much.

> August 27, 1920
> Dear Madam,
> In reply to your letter of the 14th August, I beg to inform you that the present wireless station at Cape Lazo is the property of the Dominion Government, I regret to say we know nothing about the company to which you refer and with whom you invested your money.
> G.J. Desbarats
> Deputy Minister

It would seem that Mrs. Bauer may have been bamboozled into investing in a non-existent company.

---

[81] The Marconi station, XWA, had started experimental broadcasts the winter before; it was the first station to be licenced in Canada, September 1919.

Canada led the way in clearing up ship interference to broadcast radio by signing treaties with 10 other countries. For instance, when spark transmitters were found to cause a great deal of interference, the change to new tube equipment was accelerated. Also, as early as 1925, Canada forced ships in its waters to stop using just any wave in the broadcast band. Similar arrangements existed with the United States and later stood as the blueprint for international regulations. At the Washington International Radio Convention of 1927, where 76 different administrations were represented, Canadian policy earned international prominence.

Interference Call

Still in the early 1920s, all of the 37 coast stations in Canada as well as the land station at Le Pas, Manitoba, were owned by the Canadian government. Seventeen were directly operated by the Department of the Naval Service, including the west coast stations and the coast stations along Hudson Bay; Halifax and Barrington Passage, Nova Scotia; and the four direction-finding stations along the east coast at Canso, Yarmouth, St. Paul Island and Cape Race. The other 20 stations were operated by the Marconi Wireless Company of Canada under contract to the Canadian government and were situated on the Great Lakes and on the east coast. The total revenue generated by these stations in 1922 was $54,161.76. With the ever-increasing number of amateur and public broadcast stations coming online in the first half of the century, the problem of interference again surfaced. Radio was overstepping itself at a maddening rate. The government scrambled to keep pace.

As early as 1912, radio interference on the west coast posed a serious problem. At the time, it was thought that the cause of the interference was directly related to the escalating number of ship stations and the operation of several additional American stations on the shores of Puget Sound, just south of Vancouver. Little could be done to prevent the interference. In the meantime, government and commercial stations in both countries agreed to operate in respective 30-minute blocks.

The 1912 Annual Naval Service Report states that "the geographical position of the stations on the east coast renders that service practically immune from interference by foreign stations, but the trouble we now encounter on the west coast will be met on the Great Lakes immediately after that service is placed in operation." The report continues, however, to state that "the difficulty is not insurmountable, it can be overcome to a great extent by accurate tuning, differentiation of wavelengths and powers to be used at the individual stations concerned."

Almost 10 years later, in 1921, the Inductive Interference Section released a summary of its research findings.[82]

The number of large generators at the stations had been causing the interference for many years. Finally, after much investigation and testing, the department determined what suppression devices and methods to use.

The average noise level in many districts had been significantly reduced by eliminating many sources of long-standing interference caused by telephone and telegraph distribution systems and privately owned apparatus.

Increased maintenance of lines and equipment belonging to public utilities greatly cut down the intermittent interference. Improved transmitting and receiving equipment as well as wiring also contributed to the decline of the nagging interference.

Manufacturers played an important role in reducing interference as well. They were constantly improving their equipment designs and cooperating with the Department of Marine and Fisheries Radio Branch to cut down the distribution of interference-causing equipment.

By the same token, the interference caused by amateur stations was overcome by strict enforcement of the licence clause of the *Telegraphs Act*. Amateur radio operators had discovered that the bottom portion of the high-frequency band was of some use for communications. With the increased interference resulting from the popularity of communications, official or otherwise, amateur radio enthusiasts were forced to broadcast outside those areas of the spectrum which were considered the most useful for long-distance communication. International regulators permitted amateur wavelengths shorter than 200 metres (1,500 kHz).[83] Prior to these imposed restrictions, all frequencies above our present AM broadcast band were considered useless. Progress along these lines clearly indicated that all it would take to make full use of higher frequencies was a better vacuum tube. Communications on high frequencies, which produced continuous waves of very long range with fairly low power, were not only possible but practical.

Amateurs had to take the regulations in stride and agree to operate using a wavelength shorter than 200 metres, that is to say 50 metres in most cases, allowing only a maximum power of 500 watts—giving a very low, 25-kilometre range. Under the regulations, the wavelengths used varied according to the distance between the licensed station and any

---

[82] Department of Marine and Fisheries Annual Report for the end of the fiscal year 1921.
[83] Ibid., p. 50.

commercial or land station or route of navigation. Regulators enforced this rule so that amateur stations did not interfere with the standard wavelengths of 300 and 600 metres. By 1920, there were 281 licensed amateur radiotelegraph stations in Canada.

1920 Amateur Wavelength Restrictions

Within five miles	50 metres
Between five and 25 miles	100 metres
Between 25 and 75 miles	150 metres
More than 75 miles	200 metres

During the winter of 1921, the Department of Marine and Fisheries gave all amateur radio operators from Port Arthur, Ontario, to Québec City, permission to use a transmitting wavelength of 200 metres during the navigation off-season. The experiment was conducted to determine the resulting interference and, generally speaking, it was a success—while interference was generated at some stations, in most cases it was due to badly tuned sets. Tests did continue, however, to ascertain what policies were needed to govern wavelength limitations for amateur radio stations. The 1912 Naval Service report, signed by Deputy Minister C.P. Edwards, states that "it will be readily understood that any drastic suppression of such stations will be a great detriment to the advance of the art of wireless telegraphy in this country..." There is some foretelling in the statement if we consider that amateur radio operators were the first to recognize the importance of the bottom portion of the high-frequency band.

In 1923, the year after the Radiotelegraph Service was transferred back to the Department of Marine and Fisheries, longer wavelengths for experimental or amateur stations became available. Amateur stations could transmit on the following wavelengths:
- Pure CW—all waves in the band 125 to 150 metres, 175 metres, and all waves in the band 200 to 225 metres.
- Spark—175 metres only.
- Radiophone and ICW—wavelengths of 150, 175 and 200 metres.
- Experimental stations were allowed to transmit on all the above wavelengths and on 275 metres for special experimental work.

Radiotelephone broadcasting was one of the more notable developments in telecommunications technology in 1923 and, from a public standpoint, it was most interesting because of its application to broadcasting. To wit, 62 licences were granted that year alone. The stations varied in range from local stations with a radius of 16 kilometres to those with a radius of 415 kilometres. The wavelength band reserved for broadcasting was 400-450 metres. No other radio work was allowed on this wavelength. The popularity of broadcasting continued unabated. The Department of Marine and Fisheries adhered to the stipulations set down in the *Radio Act* of 1913. In 1924, there were 46 broadcasting stations in Canada and 600 in the United States. It is interesting that, indirectly, the predecessor of the Canadian Radio-Television and Telecommunications Commission (CRTC) was a department responsible for oceans and fisheries.

There was a growing tendency in the U.S. to place high-power stations on these higher frequencies because of congestion in the upper bands. The question of the specific division of these frequencies between the two countries was dealt with later.

Estevan Point and World War II

Japanese submarines were active along the North American west coast during the Second World War, some of which were spotted in Victoria. The subsequent incendiary shellings of American forests were attributed to these submarines. On June 20, 1942, it was an especially beautiful day. It was just after Father's Day when Brian Harrison, a Canadian radio operator, had his first-born child in his arms and was making his way back to the station following an afternoon picnic. He and the officer in charge, E.T. Redford, were heading toward the Estevan Point station when suddenly they heard a horrible noise. Redford, a World War I veteran, recognized it immediately. A Japanese submarine was shelling the Estevan Point lighthouse. In the meantime, Bob Glass, another operator, told his wife to stay in the house while he pulled the switch to douse the lights, and Vern Read, the operator on watch, signalled that the station was under attack and was closing until further notice. The shelling lasted about 20 minutes. The staff stayed in the woods while 5.8" armour-piercing shells smashed into the vicinity of the station.

The deck of the submarine was filled with machine guns and the crew had apparently been ordered to expend munitions as they saw fit. At least that is what they reported when the submarine was seized by Allied Forces in the South Pacific.

Most of the shells fell short of their target and landed on the beach. The submarine raised its sights and then shot high with most of the shells exploding in the woods behind the station. The first shots, which ricocheted off the beach rocks, caused most of the damage. Personnel later assessed the damage and, minor as it was, the crack in the cement of the tower of the lighthouse and shattered glass from the prism were proof of an unforgettable ordeal.

Later, to offer some security to the employees and their families, the Department of Defence handed out very used Lee-Enfield 303-calibre rifles to the coast-station staff. The government also offered, to those who wanted them, transfers out of the area. Most of the operators waited for regular transfers, but the wives and children left. Historian Desmond Morton wrote:

> The Pacific War had little impact on Canada. Invasion, service commanders patiently explained, was physically impossible. A single Japanese submarine lobbed a few shells at the Estevan Lighthouse and fled, after the first and only direct enemy attack on Canadian soil since 1814. It was the indirect impact that mattered.[84]

When the shelling was first reported, it was unclear whether it was a submarine or a boat; even the number of enemy craft had yet to be established. The shelling lasted 40 minutes. Some purport that it came from a Canadian vessel, to prompt Canada into the war in the Pacific. By all accounts, the Estevan Point population took to the forest, and the neighbouring Hesquiat natives took shelter in their canoes in Hesquiat Harbour, 10 kilometres away.

Vancouver / Women Join the Team

The Second World War had an impact on more than the Estevan Point station. Point Grey, which opened in 1908, the predecessor to the Vancouver MCTS centre, gained some prominence during the war when female operators were hired to work at the station. A shortage of operators had become a serious problem and extra operators were needed as the government strove to intercept the Japanese code, commonly referred to as the KANA code.

In 1943-44, Elizabeth King took her course along with two other women. It was the thrilling "newness" of radio that attracted her. Unlike many operators at the time she did not enroll in the radio course taught by the much-revered and colourful Walter Lambert in Room 19. Apparently, the Sprott Shaw School was more tolerant of prospective female operators than was Lambert.

---

[84] Morton, Desmond. *A Military History of Canada*. Edmonton: Hurtig Publishers, 1985, p.188.

In 1941, the National Research Council (NRC) also began training women to operate high-end technology. The NRC was developing radar equipment for the Department of Defence at the time. The council trained "a nucleus of the expert maintenance staff on each new type of equipment developed by the Radio Branch." At the time, eight women were transferred from their positions as secretaries or stenographers in the Radio Branch and were given a short course on the operation of leading-edge radar equipment. The experiment was so successful that the Joint Inspection Board of the United Kingdom and Canada decided to keep the women operators on for the final testing of the GL Mk.III.C., prototype radar equipment slated for future development. Ten women were later trained to operate the GK.[85]

At war's end, the women were relieved of their duties to make way for returning veterans. "We didn't descry it at all. These were the times," says King. Most licensed female operators took to the sea aboard Norwegian vessels where attitudes toward female crew members differed greatly from the strict rigidity of other nations' merchant navies. It is not unusual on Norwegian vessels to see the captain's wife on the crew list.

In 1956, the Point Grey station was closed and its operations were amalgamated with the air services at Vancouver International Airport—the Transport Canada terminal. In 1971, the coast services moved again, but this time just to the air traffic control sector in the south terminal. The station operated as such until 1996 when its services were moved to Kap 100 in West Vancouver. Morse code, however, remained active at the south terminal. Vancouver, VAI, currently controls communications sites at Lulu Island, Bowen Island, Mount Parke, Watts Point, Howe Sound and Mount Helmcken.

---

85 *The War History of the Radio Branch*, National Research Council of Canada, Radio Branch, (Ottawa: Report no. ERA-141, unclassified, August 1948), p. 14. Directorate of History, Department of National Defense.

Chapter 7

Safe Passage—Clean Seas: Marine Communications and Traffic Services

In the 1990s, discussions of Canadian marine radio stations naturally includes the subject of Vessel Traffic Services (VTS). The integration of marine radio and VTS appeared the logical solution after the inception of the 1967 Vessel Traffic Centre, in Québec City. But it was not until 1992, when the Canadian Association of Professional Radio Operators (CAPRO) reintroduced the idea in its report *Marine Safety: A Vision for the Future*, that the idea gained real momentum. A number of recommendations in this report were rejected, however. For instance, CAPRO's proposal to combine marine radio services with Search and Rescue and with Environmental Response and Emergency Planning, did not seem feasible due to administrative and operational disparities. Complications stemmed from the fact that Search and Rescue was part of the Department of National Defence's mandate. Integration of marine communications and Vessel Traffic Services, however, did prove possible and viable.

In 1993, then Coast Guard Commissioner Michael A.H. Turner directed a committee to examine all aspects of the integration of Coast Guard Radio Services (CGRS) with Vessel Traffic Services.[86] The Committee's working groups reported to L. Humphries, Director General of Newfoundland Region. Combining these services meant a potential consolidation of 29 CGRS and 15 VTS centres, located in the six Coast Guard regions across Canada. Also considered was the effect that combining services would have on Canada's 300 radio operators and 260 vessel traffic officers. One result was certain: employees would have a

---

86 MCTS Integration National Master Plan Part II, June 1995.

$240-million surveillance and communications network with which to ply their trades.[87] Based on the report submitted by the committee on November 8, 1993, Coast Guard senior management decided to proceed with the integration, which was projected to take place gradually over a five-year period.

Safety and service were also dominant issues surrounding the integration plan. The underlying theme in the proposal suggested that with a new and united administration, efforts could be directed at modernization, greater efficiency and maintaining a par with the organization models adopted by other leading nations.

The integration of VTS and CGRS has since reduced the number of operational centres from 43 to 22, resulting in an almost 50-percent cost reduction across Canada.[88] The organizational structure in the regions necessarily had to become more streamlined and consistent, at both the operational and administrative levels. Downsizing was not easy, but it meant significant savings without compromising the effectiveness of the overall network. Extensive cross-training began and, although there are costs to bear, studies predict reduced operating expenses of about $13 million, significantly outweighing the short-term implementation costs.

The need for vessel traffic services was called to the government's attention because of safety concerns following marine incidents resulting from rising traffic volumes following the opening of the St. Lawrence Seaway. Prior to VTS, however, a marine information system had been used, which disseminated data to ship owners, agents and pilots. The St. Lawrence River-Waterways Marine Traffic Regulations were introduced. And in 1968, a radio and radar system was installed at Montréal Harbour and a small VTS in Les Escoumins. In the next decade, a national VTS program was created.

Ecareg and VTS

In the late 1970s, the heads of the Coast Guard's administration and its three regions bordering the Gulf of St. Lawrence agreed to draft and implement a set of procedures delegating regional responsibilities for ice, search and rescue, ship safety and VTS within the gulf waters. Eastern Canada Vessel Traffic Services Regulations (ECAREG) established that 66W, for example, is the point of responsibility transfer from the

---

[87] VTS/CGRS Capital Portfolio Investment Plan, amount obtained by adding the worth of both the civil works and equipment, June 1994.

[88] MCTS Integration Part I, Summary Report.

Newfoundland Region to the Laurentian Region. Similar regulations were implemented in the North and in the Pacific region in the 1980s.

ECAREG was instituted to support Vessel Traffic Services, and ensure safety and environmental protection. Vessel masters must report any defect in their ship's hull, main propulsion or steering systems, radar, compasses, radio equipment, anchors or cables that could be detrimental to safe navigation. Defects must be reported 24 hours prior to the point of entry into each VTS zone. Such regulations are essential given the aging condition of the world's merchant navy fleet. The situation is exacerbated by ship owners who cut corners by, for example, hiring crews that would not necessarily meet established North American standards. Many ocean-going ships are under Liberian registry because of Liberia's more relaxed standards, and the possibility of significant savings. These facts alone contribute to the lowering of navigation standards the world over. Establishing standards in one country is no easy matter but add to that the need to represent the interests of several nations and the task of creating international standards is daunting indeed. However, until international standards come into being, Vessel Traffic Services and complementary policies continue to ensure safety and environmental protection.

One ship in particular acted as the catalyst for the establishment of VTS systems across Canada. On February 4, 1970, the Liberian tanker, the *Arrow*, with international call sign 5LHI, ran aground at Chedabucto Bay, Nova Scotia. Cyrill Dicks, a radio operator working the Canso radio station at the time, remembers the incident well. The ship was caught on Cerberus rock.

The captain called in: "This is the *Arrow*, I am caught on a rock. Stand by."

Dicks turned to his officer in charge and said, "Captain says he's caught on Cerberus rock, he's trying to get off."

"He won't, no one ever has," the officer answered.

"This is Canso Coast Guard Radio. Do you need assistance?" the operators fired back.

"No."

Moments later another call came in. "This is the *Arrow* I am sinking."

No lives were lost, but another kind of tragedy resulted from the incident—an oil spill of rarely seen proportions. And for many months after, radio operators at Canso and other stations helped in coordinating the full-scale clean-up. The incident prompted the Canadian government to create marine traffic centres around the country to control ship movement across the various traffic zones. From the success of the Québec City and Montréal installations and the growing public calls for environmental protection, came a regular program of expansion. Included in this expansion program were systems at St. John's, Sarnia, Placentia Bay, Halifax, Saint John, Port-aux-Basques, Vancouver, Tofino and Prince Rupert. As a result of the *Arrow* incident, the Canso VTS centre opened at Eddy Point in the early 1970s.

One site chosen for these Vessel Traffic Management stations was the old Chebucto Head direction-finder site, first opened in 1917 with call sign VAV. The traffic management centre officially opened in October, 1972. When Vessel Traffic Management came into being, the fully automatic direction finder covered the VHF bands only, and when a ship was heard on the direction finder, the bearing automatically appeared on a digital display screen. Radar equipment at various sites around the area were fed into this station on closed-circuit television monitors. Certainly, the overwhelming expense to set up the network was justified. Even one of the busiest ports in the world—New York City—saw construction of a similar centre for its harbour area.

The emergence of these traffic centres across Canada introduced into the public's mind the notion of "Land Morality" and "Sea Morality"—concepts often dramatized in Joseph Conrad's popular sea stories—and the differences between them. It is common knowledge among mariners that a ship master's primary obligation is to get the ship from point A to point B, anyway he or she can. And to do that, captains have traditionally relied on the only skills available to them—their own and those of their crews—with as little help from land as possible. For centuries, mariner culture has been hued with this principle. What, then, would captains say to shore-based assistance advising them where and when to go, and perhaps even when to weigh anchor? Suffice it to say that, initially, the traffic system was not met with opposition, but with outright indifference, which in many cases is far worse. Although resolved later, conflicts arose between the age-old profession of navigation and this upstart service. A Canadian ship's radio officer recalls when the system was first put in place in the Halifax Harbour:

> At the onset there were a few bugs to iron out. The first years it was in service I never did receive a clearance to enter, until we had entered and in some cases departed. Most of the captains I sailed with could not have cared less. But I remember one who insisted on the clearance before arrival. Another Captain even told me they would be

great for running up and down the coast in fog when little navigational equipment was working. I could tell by the way he told me this that he already knew how he would extract his position from these regulators without admitting his navigational equipment was down.[89]

Many captains felt that their work was being infringed upon, and it took several years before the system gained any widespread acceptance. Ronald Landry, an operator and a regulator,[90] knows the reticence that ship masters felt towards the pioneering technology. The following is a portion of the communication he held with a Captain plying the St. Lawrence.

"Listen, I am the captain aboard this ship and I intend to do as I wish."

"Listen Captain," retorts Landry who at this point is fraught with fatigue, "I am the master over the St. Lawrence and I intend that you do as *I* wish. Please acknowledge."

(Static-filled pause) "Roger," the captain finally muffled back.

While Landry's outburst was humourous, it was not condoned. In retrospect, though, he feels that in some small way, it helped establish respect for the St. Lawrence Traffic system.

With the new equipment and procedures now in place, blinding rainstorms and dense fogs hinder traffic movements only minimally when compared with the harrowing conditions under which ships blindly sailed in the past. Collisions were not rare but, with Vessel Traffic Services operational, captains now have an extra margin of safety. It is widely known that for most of our history, the St. Lawrence has posed navigational difficulties. Its high banks, winding length and narrow channel coupled with swelling traffic made shore-based navigation assistance vital.

The original Montréal/Québec City system consisted of a channel display and XY digital plotter graphically showing the status of all shipping along some 415 kilometres of the St. Lawrence. The system included some automated elements such as the Honeywell DDP-516 computer, four controllers' consoles and a supervisor's console, VHF communication control units, teletypes, telephones and eight weather display units.[91] "I like to think of it as an air-traffic system in a marine environment," said Captain George G. Leask, former chief of the marine

---

[89] Spurgeon Roscoe, *Radio Stations Common? Not This Kind*, 1981.

[90] Regulators or radio operators are now trained to work both vessel traffic and radio communications. The designated term is now MCTS Officer.

[91] Honeywell brochure on the pioneering system, circa 1970.

traffic control operation in the Laurentian Region. Leask is absolutely correct. In fact, the principles of air-traffic control were transferred directly to this completely new marine traffic environment. Radar would be added to the traffic system later. The system was hailed as the most important innovation in the history of navigation in this country. Initially, the service was put in place to avoid collisions and to assure safe, rapid, efficient navigation. But most importantly, it serves to warn appropriate agencies in case of distress. To this end, the St. Lawrence was divided into four sections with Québec City acting as the control centre for three of the four. The control centre for the fourth section is now in Longueuil, Québec, a suburb of Montréal. A 24-hour service links ships to shore via a VHF radio network.

Progress in vessel traffic systems continued with the conditional acceptance of the West Coast system with five radar sites and automatic target tracking, and the installation, in 1982, of a new radar surveillance system at Les Escoumins, Québec. Until then, most VTS radar and display systems were adaptations of shipboard equipment or scaled-down air-traffic control units. But around the world, various companies were designing new systems, specifically with VTS requirements in mind. The Norwegian company, Norcontrol, became a world leader in this field.

Due notification by Notices to Mariners was given and the overall marine traffic control system came into being on April 3, 1967—a world first in terms of an integrated system of policies, standards, procedures and equipment based on a national vision and direction.

Québec

Before 1967, Québec City already had a rich marine radio history. By 1910, a web of wireless stations had spread rapidly along the St. Lawrence River, the Gulf of St. Lawrence and the Atlantic coast. Twenty-nine stations were operating, forming a full communication chain and offering ships unprecedented shore assistance. Around the same time, the Québec City station, VCC, along with Port Menier at Anticosti Island and Grosse-Île, came into being. One year later, both the Québec and Grosse-Île stations, initially commissioned by the Public Works Department, were transferred to the Department of Naval Service. Operations at the stations were later assumed by the Marconi Wireless Company.

In 1914, a suitable site for an enlarged station at Québec City was secured in the old part of the city, to the west of the Citadel. The Department of Militia and Defence, which controlled the property, granted the necessary permission. But owing to objections raised by the local community, the work was delayed. No records were found to explain what, exactly, the community objected to. However the station opened some months later, including a new transmitting apparatus of two kilowatts, the industry standard of the day. The set operated from the city supply and a musical spark was obtained by means of a non-synchronous disc discharger—the total cost incurred for the new installation was $895.74.

On August 4, 1914, VCC and all other radiotelegraph stations in Canada were placed on war duty—that is to say, all marine radio stations were transferred to the Naval Service. A trend was set for the Second World War.

Decades later, the increased use of radiotelephony by vessels in the St. Lawrence Seaway revealed that coverage was not sufficient in the section between Montréal and Québec City. A survey was undertaken in 1954 confirming the dead spots. The result was a new station at Trois-Rivières, on the site of an old Marconi station, under the call sign VCB.

In 1956, at the time when the Department of Transport was taking over Marconi stations and both air and marine services were being integrated, Québec City, VCC, was moved to the Ancienne-Lorette Airport, a Québec City suburb. On April 1, 1979, marine radio operations at the Ancienne-Lorette Airport were closed and moved to Québec City. A few years later, on February 4, 1984, the Québec City Telecom & Electronics staff and operations were moved from *Place Québec* to the new Pratt Building on Dalhousie Street. The Québec City Vessel Traffic Service, along with all others across the country, were officially integrated with marine communications in 1996. Now, the Québec City MCTS centre operates from the Canadian Coast Guard base on Champlain Boulevard.

Montréal

Montréal, the second location to boast a VTS centre, 1968, came into its own early on with stations constructed at a variety of locations. First, the location of the station at Tarte Pier, section 44 of today's Port of Montréal, had long been considered an unfavourable site for receiving. Induction from the high-tension power lines in the vicinity had become so intense that in 1914 it was decided to move to a new site. In 1914, a suitable site for the proposed new station at Montréal was secured in St. Michel de Laval. The total area of the site was "nine arpents and the purchase price was $1,400 per arpent."[92] Because of more pressing war-related work, construction of the new operating house was delayed until August 1, 1921, and the new installation opened on October 10, 1921.

After World War II, radio communications formerly operated by the Royal Air Force (RAF) were taken over by the Department of Transport and used to disseminate and collect meteorological information pertaining to transatlantic flights. The Montréal station communicated with Prestwick in Scotland, the Azores, Bermuda, Gander and Goose Bay, Labrador. The expanded activity forced the reopening of a station on Tachereau Boulevard near St. Lambert, Québec—formerly used to serve the St. Hubert Airport. The direction-finding station operated by the RAF at Goose Bay, together with all radio equipment, was also taken over by the Department of Transport.

The growth of radiotelephony and radiotelegraphy and Omni Range radio beacons increased the department's responsibilities. Added to these were new responsibilities associated with military stations-cum-Department of Transport stations. The increase in responsibilities prompted the opening of regional offices across the country. In 1946, a departmental office thus opened in Montréal to serve a new district covering the area from Montréal to Baie des Chaleurs, Québec.

The aeradio and marine radio installations at Montréal were combined into a single entity at the Dorval Airport in 1961. The Trois-Rivières station was later closed due to redundancy, and its services were integrated at Montréal in 1978.

In 1990, all segments of the Coast Guard, Montréal region, were united under one roof at 101 Rolland Terrien Boulevard in the suburb of Longueuil. The new regional centre became the home for all radio personnel from the Coast Guard station at Dorval, including traffic officers from the VTS centre at the Sutherland dock.

LORAN

In 1961, the Department of Transport decommissioned the Québec Decca Navigator Chain and planned its relocation to cover the Gulf of St. Lawrence, the St. Lawrence River and the Saguenay River. Specifications were issued to regulate the removal of the electronic equipment to storage and for the construction of 91-metre vertical radiators, using a new method of top-loading to obtain high efficiency. The second chain closed

---

[92] An old French measurement of land area, formerly used in Canada, equal to about 3,400 square metres.

later in March, 1984, in favour of LORAN[93] technology. The LORAN-C system and a new installation at Fox Harbour ensured complete coverage of the east coast of the country.

In September, 1977, a jointly funded Canada-U.S. Canadian LORAN-C chain was inaugurated on the Canadian west coast. The master station was built at Williams Lake, British Columbia, and the secondary stations were built in Alaska and Washington State. More LORAN-C stations were opened on the east coast in May, 1980, marking the end of Decca and LORAN-A technology altogether. A LORAN station had existed at Battle Harbour, Labrador, where the degree of interference and cross-modulation was such that point-to-point communications and private correspondence could be picked up on broadcast radios in nearby southern Labrador villages. If, for instance, someone had an embarrassing medical problem and discussed it on the airwaves with a doctor, the whole southern coast of Labrador was soon in the know.

DGPS

The more position-finding systems there were, the more doubt there was concerning the future of many Coast Guard radio stations. Put in service in 1993 by the U.S. Department of Defense, the Global Positioning System (GPS) enables mariners to obtain positions within a 100-metre tolerance. The administrative body of GPS oversaw the production and maintenance of 21 satellite vehicles, plus three active spares, to provide continuous, worldwide navigation services. Now, the new Differential Global Positioning System (DGPS) provides improved accuracy by using a reference GPS receiver located at a surveyed point. By comparing the coordinates of the known location and those predicted by the GPS satellite range, corrections can be determined and broadcast by a radio link to nearby users who use the corrections to calculate their position to within 10 metres.

DGPS overcomes most of the errors and problems inherent in standard positioning services, mainly the satellite clock and factors such as ionospheric noise. DGPS can work in all areas and in all kinds of weather. The corrections can also provide precision on speed, heading

---

[93] LORAN—Long Range Aid to Navigation—is a position-finding system based on determining the difference between arrival times of pulse-type radio signals transmitted between a triad of stations. The time differences are measured on a receiver and used in conjunction with specially prepared charts and tables to establish lines of position. The intersection of two or more lines of position, determined from two or more pairs of stations, provided the required position.

and distances to way-points. A marine DGPS end-user system requires little modification to ship-borne equipment, and allows for the use of existing radio beacon transmission stations.

Suez, Supertankers and MCTS

The story of marine radio communications and of VTS in Canada reveals a commitment and level of expertise of which any nation would be proud. Canada's pioneering efforts in the field have not gone unnoticed. In autumn, 1996, a Canadian Coast Guard team travelled to Egypt to develop an implementation plan for a Vessel Traffic Services system in the Gulf of Suez. The project was the result of a request by the International Maritime Organization (IMO) which, according to Spencer Martin, Chief of Operations and Procedures, is a special vote of confidence in Canadian expertise.

In Egypt, the Gulf of Suez represents a crucial point for attracting foreign business. The region is the site of three important industries, including tourism, petroleum production and navigation on the Suez Canal. From supertankers to pleasure craft, vessels plying the canal are many and of all kinds. And the Egyptian government is conscious of the repercussions that can arise from a maritime disaster. To avoid mishap, it is now prepared to invest significant resources to safeguard its essential economic activities.

Vessel Traffic Services play a crucial role in preventing collisions and groundings on waterways—at once ensuring the movement of vessel traffic and preventing possible problems. The VTS system is comprised of three primary elements: radio communication with vessels, radar surveillance and shore-based coordination made possible by "an infrastructure of staff, policies, procedures and physical structures and systems."[94] The Egyptian government views a modern VTS system as a critical part of the safety system required in the Gulf of Suez.

> Foreign projects are a good learning experience for CCG personnel, providing an urgent incentive to keep abreast of developments elsewhere. Unfortunately, we can no longer claim to be at the cutting edge of technology when speaking of MCTS. Foreign projects provide a mechanism and funds to undertake studies and technology investigations, which we might not do so quickly under normal circumstances, due to budget limitations. Visiting foreign

---

[94] Spencer Martin, "From Supertankers to Sailboats: Managing Vessel Traffic in the Gulf of Suez," *Echo* (Canadian Coast Guard, Jan-Feb. 1997), p. 4.

ports gives us a sense of perspective, as well as educating us on the many and varied reasons why VTS is established in countries around the world. When we come to the point where we must review levels of service, the experience of other countries can help us make enlightened choices.[95]

100 Years of Service

Sir Wilfrid Laurier and William Mulock (Canada's first Postmaster General) would no doubt agree that marine radio stations such as Point Grey, gave Canada the wherewithal to govern its vast territory. With both men and women at the consoles, the service has been maintained, largely uninterrupted, for nearly 100 years. The next millennium will likely bring even more benefits resulting from the ever-improving communications technologies. It is safe to say, however, that it all truly began when Marconi received the first transatlantic message in Newfoundland, Canada.

More than 100 years after Marconi's first efforts in the now-burgeoning field of telecommunications, marine radio as we know it no longer encircles the globe. And much like lighthouses, radio's hand in economic development has not yet been fully appreciated. Statistics can justify why the St. Lawrence River was long held an emblem of navigational hazards, being the most treacherous waterway to navigate in the 18th and 19th centuries. Some measure of guidance came with the advent of lighthouses in the 19th century. But real risk reduction was provided by marine radio in the 20th century, no longer requiring mariners to be within sight of succour to rest easier. Marconi first brought the candle into the unlit room of navigation, and radio operators ever since, with their seemingly indelible bond with the sea, have kept that candle burning.

As a new millennium approaches, a significant chapter of maritime history comes to a close. New challenges will come, leaving behind more traditional modes of communication that have, for decades, sounded with letters and voices, moving "across the void or a shore station, solemn and purposeful like the voice of God. . ."[96] The methods, though part of tradition, are in perpetual movement. From Spark to CW to AM, FM and Single Side Band, to today's sweeping Global Maritime Distress and

---

[95] Lea Barker, "Why We Pursue Foreign Projects," *Contact* (Ottawa: Marine Communications and Traffic Services, Canadian Coast Guard, Department of Fisheries and Oceans, March 1996, vol. I, no. 3), pp. 6-7.

[96] Thomas Raddall, *Nymph and the Lamp*.

Safety System, transition quickly gives way to nostalgia. Automated communications may have none of the romantic aspects of a "Sparks," sending code through the ether, over a tossing sea, but they do help to ensure the safety of mariners everywhere. And that, after all, has always been the goal.

Select Bibliography

Books

Brown, Richard. *Voyage of the Iceberg.* Toronto: James Lorimer & Co., 1983.

International Maritime Organization. *Solas, Consolidated Edition 1992.* London: Bath Press, 1992.

MacLeod, Mary K. *Whisper in the Air.* Hantsport, Nova Scotia: Lancelot Press, 1992.

MacNeil, Robert, et al. *The Story of English.* London: Faber and Faber, 1992.

Marsden, Michael. "Transportation in the Canadian North." William C. Wonders, ed. *Studies in Canadian Geography.* Toronto: University of Toronto Press, 1972.

Morton, Desmond. *A Military History of Canada.* Edmonton: Hurtig Publishers, 1985.

Pellegrino, Charles. *Her Name, Titanic.* New York: Avon Books, 1988.

Reid, Larry. *The Story of the West Coast Radio Service.* Vancouver: Chameleon Publishing and Graphic Design, 1992.

Smith, Henry Nash. *Virgin Land, The American West as Symbol and Myth*, Cambridge, MA: Harvard University Press, 1978.

Manuscripts

Babaian, Sharon A. *Radio Communication in Canada: An Historical and Technological Survey.* Ottawa: National Museum of Science and Technology, 1992.

Bowerman, Jack. "Early History of the Government Wireless Service on the British Columbia Coast." Victoria: Unpublished manuscript, circa 1950.

Fraser, A.H. "The Development of Radio in Canada." Address, Engineering Institute of Canada, 1930.

Radio Branch. National Research Council of Canada. *The War History of the Radio Branch*. Ottawa: Report no. ERA-141, unclassified, 1948.

Reardon, R.C. *Maritime Mobile Radio Communications and Navigation: From Marconi to Satellites*. Ottawa: Telecommunications & Electronics, Department of Transport, 1986.

Roscoe, Spurgeon. "Radio Stations Common? Not this Kind." Unpublished manuscript, 1981.

Telecommunications and Electronics Directorate. *A Short History of T & E*. Ottawa: Transport Canada, March, 1978.

Newspapers and Magazines

Baxter, J. Roy. "The Old Bard Should Have Seen Us in the North!" *News on the DOT*, Ottawa: May-June 1963.

Canada. Department of Transport. "Arctic Hub of Polar Route." *News on the DOT*, Ottawa: December 1957.

Creighton, D.G. "The Years of the Noble Experiment." *The Canadian Forum*, July 1931.

D'Onofrio, E.A. "We Heard Them Playing Autumn." *Sparks Journal*. Society of Wireless Pioneers, vol. 4, no. 4, 1982.

Gardner, Joseph V. "Traditions and Transitions." Keynote Address. *The World Wireless Beacon*. Geyserville, California: Society of Wireless Pioneers, vol. 7, no. 2, June 1995.

Gustafsson, Birgitta. "End of an 85-Year Epoch." *The World Wireless Beacon*. Geyserville, California: Society of Wireless Pioneers, vol. 7, no. 2, June 1995.

Nelson, Lloyd. "Goodbye Old Fame Point," *News on the Dot* (Ottawa: Department of Transport, December 1957), p. 2.

Sydney Daily Post. Cape Breton: January 12, 1903.

Reports

Canada. Department of Marine and Fisheries. *Marine and Fisheries Annual Report of 1908.* Ottawa: 1908.

Canada. Department of Marine and Fisheries. *Marine and Fisheries Annual Report of 1922.* Ottawa: 1922.

Canada. Department of the Naval Service. *Department of Naval Service Annual Report of 1915.* Ottawa: 1915.

Canada. Department of Transport. Telecommunications Division. *Department of Transport Annual Report of 1945.* Ottawa: 1945. (See also Department of Transport annual reports for 1951-52, 1974, 1980, 1982.)

Canada. Department of Transport. Telecommunications & Electronics Branch. *Marine Radio Communications in Canada.* Ottawa: 1968.

Canada. Gaudreau, Col. F. Department of Marine and Fisheries. *Marine and Fisheries Annual Report of 1907.* Ottawa: October 22, 1907.

Canada. Spain, O.G.V. Department of Marine and Fisheries. Canadian Marine Service. *Department of Marine and Fisheries Report.* Ottawa: December 12, 1904.

England. Department of Transport. Marine Accident Investigation Branch (MAIB). "*RMS Titanic* Reappraisal of Evidence Relating to *SS Californian.*" March 12, 1992.

About the Author

Stephan Dubreuil holds a Bachelor of Arts degree in English studies with a concentration in professional writing. He has written and translated in the fields of high technology and corporate promotion, and has contributed to the *Sherbrooke Record*. His research on marine radio involved more than two years of interviews, information gathering and writing. Stephan Dubreuil now works as a freelance writer in Montréal.